# Instill the Grain
## Oracles, Gods & Goddesses

**Zaneta Ra**

Oracle of the 144

Master of the Pearl Codes

**ISBN:** 9798376554913

Tarkington Text Press
www.angelicpearls144.com

*This book is dedicated to the god self within you, the reader. May the wisdom and light encoded in this book ignite, brighten, and expand your light. We will forever fly as one because we are all of ONE LIGHT.*

# Contents

# Introduction

Worshiping the gods is not the act of idolizing something outside of self, it is the exact opposite. Worshiping the gods is an act of honoring that which is of your wholeness. What you exist to be is that lightning bolt sent from the Heavens to Earth.

Who you are simply is the grain. You are the manifestations held within the mighty hourglass of time. You are the particles of light fractalized yet unified as material forms. Forms that you, yourself created that reside within a sandbox on a playground. You have the Divine Will to choose any sandbox you desire. You have the power of choice. You have the power to play in solitude or among those you feel drawn to.

Life itself is a playground created by the gods. Just like any playground, there is always a bully. However, this bully is your teacher hidden under a shadow mask. This playground is what helps mold your path of expansion and enlightenment. Just like any schooling, you have the power of choosing where you want to go next. Some allow their parents to choose for them. Some follow in cliques. Some are nomads, merely wiseman in the making. There is never a wrong time to choose, for even a grandparent can alter their path and choose to master a new trade.

The gods and the Elementals were created to oversee and manage all the Earthly Worlds, the *sandboxes*. If you go to the start of the Pearl Code teachings *(Angelic Pearls 144 book)*, we speak about the Alpha: Omega. Those first sparks emitted from THE MIND are most known as The Illuminated Ones, Angels, or Manifestations of The Light. These sparks were birthed from the void. That very existence outside of time and space because it is time and space. Just like your very thoughts are birthed from the void of your mind, so was existence itself.

We spoke of how the first thought emitted 144 sparks knowns as The Seraphim. 72 aspects of shadows and 72 aspects of light, the 144 Rays of Creation. The ones known in legends as the gods are themselves extensions of the 144 rays of existence. It is from the God Worlds that they projected particles of themselves into the Earthly Worlds. Souls created from them are those that stem from the 9D realms and below. These are what we term as Mortal Souls.

Those of the material planes travel throughout the Earthly Worlds to evolve and traverse. It was not until these particles of the gods started to become resistant in nature, that The Illuminated Ones were sent by Divine. This was implemented because the imbalance of energy from the Earth Worlds caused the God Worlds themselves to become unbalanced.

The god Uranos is the aspect of *above Earthly Realms,* and it was from him that the god Kronus *(Cronus)* was birthed. Kronus simply is time itself. Time was created to compartmentalize the material existence. Timelines themselves work in spirals and where they cross create portals known as time nodes. This is where selected Souls are injected to assist with balancing the energy of the Earthly Worlds.

Time along with other aspects of the gods were factualized and dispersed upon the Earthly Worlds. The god Zeus is the parental aspect of the Mortal Souls incarnated, meaning their Higher Self. The fractals of Zeus are 33, meaning his offspring seen in mythology.

These are separated fractals held within this god ray expression labelled as Zeus. The 33 stairsteps one must climb in order to reach the God Worlds, a process known as Ascension.

Light is who you are. Love simply is existence itself. You are the GRAIN molded from light into love.

### Light Is God Housed in Thyself

*Rhea gives rock to Cronus,* {{PD-US}} *by Karl Friedrich Schinkel, 19th Century*

9

*"The mortals feel drawn to us because they are us. They seek for us like a child to his parent. However, just like a child, a time will come when they turn a deaf ear upon our wisdom and guidance."*

*~Zeus*

# How to Read this Book

As you read this book you will feel a change of energy. This is due to the flow of the 144 Seraphim and their god/goddess essence flowing through me as I scribe. As an Oracle the energy shifts from I to we in every now moment. You will see references to the other Pearl books in case you are new to these teachings.

As you read with your heart you may also receive visuals and downloads of information from them. This is a coded book just like all the Pearl Code Teaching books. If you notice yourself feeling fatigue or dizzy, please take time to rest before returning to this book. The reason is due to the upgrades happening within your cellular structure. This only happens with the approval of your Higher Soul Spark.

This book is intended for the truth seekers of the gods and those on their Ascension pathway, both aware and unaware. May this book **Instill the Grain** of your Light Seed.

# Instill the Grain
### Zaneta Ra

**I**ntegration
**N**ow of
**S**elf
**T**ranscendence
**I**n
**L**ight and
**L**ove


**G**ratitude of existence
**R**espect of breath
**A**cknowledgement of sovereignty
**I**ntegrity of light
**N**eutrality of characters

{{PD-US}} *The Pleiades, Elihu Vedder, 1885*

12

# The Grain

As I walked around in nature, I heard a voice whisper to me *"Instill the Grain"*. I then stopped to connect with the source of this message. I saw a Master of Light standing in front of a doorway of bright white light. His appearance was that of golden light, and he held a tall staff with a glowing scepter atop it. As he slowly turned to point to the light, he began to sparkle with a multitude of colors. He then said again to me *"Instill the Grain"* as he pointed at the light.

This was no ordinary light for it was THE LIGHT, as in God Source. As I started to become encompassed by THE LIGHT, there was a seed crystal placed within and around me. This seed crystal was the very grain that God Source asked me to plant upon the Earthly Worlds.

At that moment I was reminded of my Angelic duties and asked to share some of my experiences to the world. I was asked to explain what incarnated Angels do, why we are here in the flesh, and our connection to the gods and Oracles.

# Christos Angels

In the beginning, Source split into two energies which are most known as The Mind or as Divine Masculine and Divine Feminine. When the initial split occurred, 144 sparks of light emitted, which are known as the Seraphim. The next stage was to create more sparks of light known as Angels. It was during these stages that God Source instilled light crystals in select Angels. These light crystals are known upon this plane as the Christ Seed or the Christos Egg.

These light crystals are the Christos Keys of Creation. They are keys that allow these Angels to access all Kingdoms as well as all Divine Blueprints. An Angel simply is a messenger of THE LIGHT. However, each messenger holds a different elixir that God Source created them upon. Each elixir was created directly from God Source with specific light sparks that hold an exact imprint of expression. This expression is known as the *message* that God Source designed that Angel to anchor into the Kingdoms of Creation.

Each message *(Angel)* is sent out per Divine Will into a specific time space reality held within a Kingdom. When it comes to the Earthly Kingdoms, Angels incarnate to anchor Light Codes that help to expand the human collective consciousness. These Light Codes are plasma sparks of light encoded with a specific vibrational octave that can be equivalent to a music note. That music note can be seen as a key to a song sheet. The song sheet is the organic blueprint of that specific time note.

These time nodes are known as the Ascension Gateways. That specific time node when the light and shadow aspects of Creation are out of balance and can no longer coexist. This coexistence is known as polarity. Polarity exists within all the Earthly Kingdoms and are Divinely Designed to be balanced. It is not until they become out of alignment does a Gateway occur.

Polarity itself was created to act as a positive and negative charge of a dimensional field of existence. God Source energy is fed into the North field, osculates clockwise inside of that space, and then exits the South field. If the balance is off, the energy meets resistance which causes an imbalance in the natural flow of God Sources energy. This is likened to the flow of a river. Hence why life is seen as a river and all of Creation is designed to simply flow as one with it.

The positive field is seen as the light aspect of Creation, where the negative field is seen as the shadow aspect. There always comes a time when particles of existence gain more energy and start to accelerate at fast speeds. They become ready to shift into the next stage. They become ready to be reborn and that creates a Gateway.

The particle is seen here as the Earthly Kingdom. Its essence is birthing anew and not all energies are going with her. This new aspect of her being shifted can be seen as a new layer developing on an onion. It is during this birthing stage that the unbalanced energies have an opportunity to shift as well. This is when the Angels come into play.

The Higher essence of a Soul incarnated sends out a signal that it wants to shift into the next higher octave of existence. While incarnated, it will have several Masters of Light as well as Masters of Shadows enter its field. The incarnated aspect is known as the Lower Self. The Lower Self has free will over the energy fusion it desires to play with.

The role of the incarnated Angels varies but when it comes to the Ascension Angels, they have the same duties. Their main duty is to be the pure vessel of God Source. Their devotion to service holds no free will and their mission during this incarnation is to spread THE LIGHT. This is done in endless ways and our work never ends. We were created to do this for all eternity, and it is our passion.

We come in to be an anchor point so the energy from the Higher Realms can feed through us into this plane via our energy fields. Our energy field acts as a portal system for specific Light Codes to filter through. They filter into all the Earthly grids so others can access this energy. Each grid is of a specific vibration. In order to access that field, one must be a vibrational match. Each field stores information like a celestial library.

When one goes into meditation or simply when their consciousness field has ascended into the next octave, they can access a new field of information. This new field provides them with an entirely new perspective on life and existence itself. This is what happens when you wake up and see things in a completely different light. Things, people, food etc. that you once aligned with, suddenly you feel disconnected to.

Another duty we have is to allow God Source and our Angelic family to speak through us to deliver Divine Messages. These messages can be seen in an endless way, some examples are:

Dancing
Literally providing messages to people
Art
Writing
Singing
Gridwork
Healing
Assisting departing Souls over (*we act as a portal home which is a messenger*)
Creating films/shows and all other creative outlets

# Seraphim

When it comes to an incarnated Seraphim, we can be seen as a direct manifestation of God Source. We come in to bring Divine Wisdom and assist the human collective consciousness field with expansion. Some prior incarnated Light Masters have said that the Seraphim are spiritual entities created with the capacities infinitely superior to the average human. That they are sent to a specific period per Divine Order, to act as an instrument of Divine intervention so that specific species can inherit its capacities of understanding who they are.

The Seraphim were created as the guardians and caretakers of existence. There are specific Seraphim families assigned to each Kingdom. When they send one of their Light Seeds to incarnate within that Kingdom, that incarnate acts on behalf of them as a unity consciousness. It is because of this that these beings are seen as highly intelligent and a library of wisdom.

Other incarnates are a Light Spark of consciousness sent on behalf of their Higher essence. It is during times of Ascension that these sparks long to reunite with their Higher essence and no longer be fragmented. This can be gained if the preselected wishes of the Higher essence have been fulfilled. Examples of why a physical Ascension doesn't take place can be:

- If that Soul preselected to reincarnate on Earth more in order to expand its light field.
- If that Soul wanted to experience a mortal physical death transition.
- If that Soul has a Divine Duty that requires more incarnations upon the Earthly Kingdom.
- If that Soul chooses to experience what it is like to be fragmented.
- If that Soul chooses to descend in elements and many more scenarios.

The Seraphim will come into form when it is time for planting seeds and when it is time for harvesting them. The Seraphim act as the Gateway Greeters for the Higher Realms. Meaning, that when it is time for you to Ascend into the God Kingdoms, we will be your first contact. There are some Soul incarnates that have not selected to enter the God Kingdoms but instead the Galactic Realms. They will have Galactic beings greet them instead.

We want it to be known that as one ascends into a new existential space, they gain more responsibilities. We have seen how the end goal taught upon Earth currently is the pure bliss stage. This is not how physical Ascension is obtained but merely a steppingstone of the phases. When one masters the identity consciousness stage, they move onto the god consciousness stage which houses the bliss phase.

This is the phase where you embody the full understanding that you are all things. It is the beautiful phase when you fully transmute that feeling of emptiness into pure bliss. That euphoric moment when you finally see that the Universe and everything else, is not outside of you but inside of you. It is that very moment when you finally feel connected to ALL again.

# Oracles

Oracles are direct manifestations of The Light sent as Divine Messengers and eyes of God Source. They are a window and a portal between this world *(Earth)* and the God Worlds *(heavens)*. When incarnated, we have one foot in the heavens and the other on Earth. This allows us to always be able to see and exists in both worlds at once.

The shape of an oculus *(window)* stems from Oracles because we are walking windows. It is because of this that when others are in our energy field, they get this feeling of home. They get charged up with energy and their psychic abilities are 3-10 times more powerful when they are in our energy fields. This can cause a codependent *(usually unconsciously)* attachment from that person because they long to feed from that energy. Oracles are no different than the ancient Priests and

Priestesses of Sacred Temples, especially Mystery Schools.

When you look at the word *Oracle* what do you see first? The word Ora. This means *mouth, speech,* and *prayer.* The word prayer describes a communicational act between humans and the Sacred God Source, gods *(Archangels),* or the transcendent realm. This originated from humans going into sacred Oracle Temples to communicate with the Higher Planes. This is seen most today in the western part of the world as communication with the Angels. The energy essence of those termed Archangels and ancient gods of

23

several religions are of the same source stream. *(See the* **God Kingdoms** *Chapter)*

The word Oracle originally was *Orakel.* Kel is where the word keld stems from which means *spring* or *fountain.* This is due to the Orakels/Oracles being the Earthly vessel for the plasma light *(densified water)* to flow through. When we look at the origin of what the term Divine Will means, it is this. Will is the spoken word of Divine. A flow of water is seen as the spoken word that flows from above to that of Earth. This is a messenger of The Light, an Angel, an Oracle, a Priest, a Priestess etc.

The word ora in Gaelic means *light.* It is this very *light,* the bio-geometric Light Codes spoken from the mouth of the ancient Sacred Priests and Priestess of those very Temples, that helped to transcend the mortal pupils. This was the origins of Ascension Temples. This was how those sacred teachings from the transcendence realms reached the humans seeking to transform out of the flesh. To ascend simply is the act of transcendence itself.

The gifts of an Oracle are mostly known as a seer, yet they house many more gifts. Oracles have all their psychic abilities fully on at the time of birth. All who incarnate with full abilities turned on are of the

Angelic realms and it is their light that activates these abilities within the human form. When it comes to psychic abilities, it does not solely pertain to the type of physical blood a human has but to the Light Body. It is the coding of ones Light Body that determines what abilities they are gifted access to. Psychic abilities are knowns as gifts because they are designed to be used to serve.

# Angel Oracles

Even though Oracles are Divine Messengers, not all Oracles are incarnated Angels. Oracles that are also Angels are sent on behalf of God Source directly for a specific mission. This is a mission they have known since childhood and have been prepared through the many realms for when God Source calls them to rise and serve.

Oracles can feel all energies of existence and are able to time walk since birth. I call it *dream walking* because to me this entire world is simply a "dream" held within The Mighty Mind of Creator. When I shift from one period of time to another, it is as if I am simply walking from one room to another directly across the hall.

25

In ancient days Oracles were also known as Priests, Priestesses, Sages, and Wisemen. The term Sage is linked to a Wiseman or a Prophet. One thing the Angels always told me was to take an English word and seek for its origin. That will help lead you to its original meaning.

Oracles have always been here because their role was designed to help teach mankind. Oracles of today have always been an Oracle in every lifetime. We made a vow and were Divinely Ordained to do this role until the Angelic Human Template was fully fulfilled.

Wisdom comes easily to us because it is all held within our Light Body. We also have a direct link to THE MIND and hear the voice of God Source at all times. This was why Mystery Schools were created, so we could teach those who desired this wisdom. These schools originally were placed not in a city but hidden far from them.

The reason they were done this way was because if the student truly was dedicated to their spiritual path, they would travel to us. Some were even placed high atop mountains. If a pupil traversed that, they were truly dedicated. Those schools still exist today only now they are hidden behind frequency.

# Mystery Schools

Mystery Schools were specifically created over energy vortex fields. As an Oracle you already are a walking portal. Now take that and multiply it over a natural energy vortex, you create a Gateway. When these schools were overtaken by negative forces, they rebuilt atop of these schools to cap off the Gateway. This kind of field allowed energy to freely stream from the Higher Realms and vice versa. However, when a shift in energy occurred upon the Earth these access points were seen as a target.

Information taught in some of these schools were done via floating light orbs. Each orb carried an assortment of light particles known as Light Codes. The codes held within them consisted of a book of wisdom. These orbs were able to be obtained through these Light Gateways. The Gateways went directly to the center of the Sun. There is where the Pearlia City of the Solar Ones reside. They feed these orbs into a diamond river that is fed into every planet in this Solar System.

These orbs associated with the Oracles are known today as crystal balls. We did not use, nor still use crystal balls, we connect with these orbs from the Sun. When tennis ball size orbs flash around you, they are particles of light sent from these orbs. They are sent per Divine request to activate Light Codes held within your Light Body. Some mistaken these as actual Angels because they do truly deliver messages of wisdom.

These orbs were later seen has being held by Christ figures and the knowledge of them became hidden and lost. They are seen as being held by a Christ figure because it is through the Christos light these orbs can be accessed. It is through them you can gain Divine Wisdom and a better understanding of existence as well as the human species.

*Salvator Mundi, 1519, Andrea Previtali, Oil on poplar wood*

The reason it is seen in art with a cross is because the cross originally was in the shape of a solar cross. This symbol merely stood for the portal to the Big Sun. The Sun references the God Portal that connects the formless worlds with the form and the form worlds with the formless *(See **The Trident and the Rose** Chapter)*. It can be seen on ancient solar artifacts as a

29

cross with either a circle around it or in the middle of a Sun.

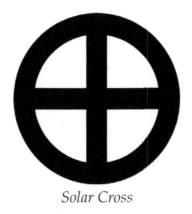

*Solar Cross*

These schools taught one everything they needed to know to expand their consciousness. Just like in the Pearl Temple schools of ancient Egypt, there were 42 Mystery Schools as well. (*For a full in depth understanding on those teachings please see the book **Rising Merits: 42 Pearl Temples of Ancient Egypt.**)*

In the image you see the Christ figure holding his fingers a certain way. This is associated with access keys to ignite the orbs. It is seen today in some movies as a way to do magic and light emits from them. This stems from the ways these orbs were accessed. However, not just anyone can access the information inside of them. Only those whose crystal heart houses the proper access keycodes can access them. The process to do this was also taught at these schools.

When it comes to what is known today as magic, it originally meant wisdom. The origin of the word *Magic* is connected to the word *Magi* which was a term for a Priest or a Priestess. It later took on the terms such as magician, sage, or wiseman. We also connect the word maga here which means *to digest*. The word maga is associated to the word magic. To really dive deep, this is where the teachings later got misconstrued to that of the womb because maga is connected to the stomach. This is when the feminine womb teachings started to surface that associated women with magic and the label "witch".

It is because of the organic teachings becoming tainted over the last 3,500 years that these Oracles as well as many other Light Masters have returned. When I was taken before The Throne of All Thrones, they showed me that 16 new timelines were created since the 1980's by those originally sent to be the Light Workers. When teachings that were originally Divinely Designed become mistaught, it opens new doorways. These new doorways create timelines that house the blueprints created by those teachings. Energy is then fed through those doorways by the Mental Bodies of those who believe in those teachings. It is only when enough energy is fed to a thought can it form into a reality.

# God Kingdoms

One of the reasons man encounters a multitude of addictions upon the Earthly worlds is so he can master it. When you enter the God Kingdoms that level of bliss and addiction becomes tenfold. This is mainly due to the enlargement of your Energy Field and the Energy Bodies held within it.

When one enters this Kingdom, they are to continue to advance and expand, however, many get stuck here due to bliss addiction. When Light Seeds expanded out from God Source, their goal was to create, learn, expand, and retract back home. The God Kingdoms are where so many aspects get halted. This is truly why many have entered the Earthly Kingdoms. The Earthly Kingdoms are all worlds that have human templates *(mainly 2D-7D)*.

The Higher essence of the Light Spark stuck within the God Kingdoms sent out another Spark to descend into the Earthly Kingdoms. This was done so that Light Spark could master discernment and temptations, then travel into the God Kingdoms to escort the stuck aspect back to its origin. This is where your true work takes place.

The God Kingdoms are where the ones known as the Immortals live. This is a heavenly place where one can choose when to be visible and invisible. This is where one can shift around the Earthly timelines and be completely invisible at will.

There are many Kingdoms here and one can morph into any form they desire. It is above these Kingdoms that the beings of pure light reside. This is in the 10th dimensional field and higher.

Each dimensional field houses several planes of existence which are known as density. It is when Earth shifts into a new dimensional field that she will no longer reside within the current Universal Field. Those who desire to shift into 5D are merely shifting into parallel timelines that is of the Galactic Worlds. This keeps one in the same dimensional field and Universal structure.

The God Kingdoms reside between the 7D and 10D existential planes. This is outside of time and space as well as this entire Universal structure. When the gateways open to this realm, it releases a formula that allows people to transform via a Spiritual Alchemy process known as a physical Ascension.

# Time Sectors

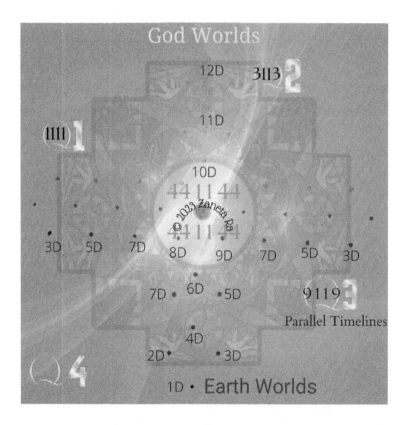

Held within this Universal structure are four Time Sector quadrants. The current Earth plane is coexisting in both the Q4 and the Q3 quad. All of humanity are existing within multiple realities and density fields at once. This causes a lot of fatigue and exhaustion on the human vessel. This is why many feel the constant roller coaster effect of life, especially since the Earthly year of 2012. This was the time node Q3 and Q4 collided.

When you look upon the image, towards the bottom right around "Earth Worlds" you will see 4D. This is currently where all of humanity resides. As you see it is in-between both quads. It also is known as the *Hall of Mirrors and Truths*. Here one can easily peak through the veil into 2D-7D, as seen on the surrounding worlds located around 4D.

4D, 6D, and 8D act as a bridge/transitional stage. It is from here one can easily move over into the 5D parallel realities or:

- Jump to 7D
- Go to the 6D bridge, then the 8D bridge, to then go on to the God Worlds
- Go to the 6D bridge, then over into the 9D Galactic Worlds of Q3
- Or descend into the 2D or 3D Worlds

There are many options one has depending on their vibrational field. The amount of energy one has within their field at the time the gates open to these options will depend on how far they can propel. This is where doing the internal work to clear any emotional/material attachments is key. The more you have anchoring you, the harder it is to propel. Remind yourself that you were not created of materials, you were created of light.

# Journey into the God Kingdoms

*Zaneta Ra:* When a guide took me into the God Kingdom that I shall call Emerald City, it triggered my memory. This was a place where no night existed. There were magical creatures you hear of in legends. So many crystalline structures and colors brighter than that of Earth. He took me to a large castle-like structure and said:

*"I am helping you remember. Just as your role there so is here it will be. You are the messenger of the gods. Our Oracle.*

*You help teach the masters selected to be. Guidance to council and to thee.*

*Mentor are you in the ways of the light. Helping guide those who have conquered the night.*

*You are the SEEer that many seek. Helping to transform those that are meek.*

*Bud into flower does your light transform. Kingdoms of all thy does adorn.*

38

*Voice of a whisper yet words of a lion.*
*Helper to see what those hath denying.*

*Rain from the Sun does thou wings bring.*
*Helping turn winter into the spring.*

*Glance in the water and thee will see. All*
*that thee conquered and all that thee be.*

*Dripped in the honey of the ALLs light.*
*Flowing with milk of the ALLs mother*
*delight. "*

When this was spoken to me, my mortal essence was not fully aware of the term "gods" in that context. I was aware that there were beings created to oversee the Material Worlds. Their realm was created in-between the Material Realms and the Celestial Realms. They can also be seen as protectors of the Gateways that lead into the access points of the Throne of All Thrones.

Throughout legends the term "gods" was used in many ways and to this day hold many definitions. In this context, however, we can view what he was speaking of is equivalent to what most call Archangels or the EL race. This is the essence most know as MichaEL, UriEL, AriEL, RaphaEL and so forth. Their essence is part of a higher Seraph form that oversees the Earthly programs. This form is the unity consciousness of the Seraphim and what I call **the 144**.

What most are not aware of is that the legends of the gods Zeus, Jupiter, Odin and even Helios, are the same essence as that of Archangel Michael. This is a hard pill for most to swallow because of the programing. This also is hard because it is so solid in the Astral Plane, which is the first field of contact for anyone who goes into meditation.

When it comes to those known as Archangels, they simply are not of a form. In their essence they merely are light. Since a child this is how I have always seen them. Any being will appear as a vibrational match to your mortal comprehension. It is not until you are no longer operating from an ego program will you see them and all of existence for its truth. Unfortunately, yet also fortunately, part of the learning process is to discern illusions and mirrors.

# The Crimson Ark

In the book *The Oresteia,* it mentions laying out a crimson tapestry for the gods to walk upon. It references that the gods' feet are unable to touch the Earth. This saying is from the ancient teachings of a crimson ark. The color crimson itself is a mixture of blue and red. Blue is the color of the blood of the gods where red is seen as the color for humans.

The true meaning of this is in order for the gods to walk upon the Earth they need a crimson ark, which is a sacred vessel. This sacred vessel is a mortal form that is sent as a manifestation of them or any Divine Vessel. A Divine Vessel is one that a messenger of God Source speaks and operates through on behalf of a Divine Mission. This is none other than an Oracle.

Oracles were seen as the Crimson Ark or the Crimson Tapestry. The word tapestry was a symbolization of a creation, in this case a sacred creation. The word tape comes from the same word origin. Tape is also something that appears like a pathway of tapestry does it not? It is laid out and used to record. This is also what an Oracle does. A role of an Oracle is also to record and be the eyes of God Source as well as of the gods. Keep in mind when we speak of the gods it is one in the same as those termed Archangels. The team of High Arks that oversee the Divine Blueprints of the Earthly Worlds.

Later when there was a shift in energy upon the Earth, there was a mission to demolish all knowledge of this and the Oracles by the negative forces. The original meaning of laying out a crimson tapestry was shifted into the blood sacrifices given to the gods. Since the origin of the word crimson was used as a reference to a sacred vessel that itself, has the bloodline of the gods running through it, we can see here how it was shifted to literally mean blood.

This was shifted to be the widespread gossip, if you will, of those times to paint these sacred beings as barbaric. Even the word barbaric at that time simply was used by the Romans to call anyone who was not of Roman blood.

# The Trident and the Rose

When it comes to the creation of the mortal worlds, there first were the worlds of the Immortals. Immortals are beings who are not bound by an Earthly vehicle such as flesh and bones. What we speak of are those known as the Gods, Masters, and Angels. It is from them that the Earthly Worlds were created. The reason the gods created that of material form was to create a moving image of eternity.

Eternity in itself is that which we label the Universe or Heaven. What resides there is truly mirrored here but with moving images that are bound by timestamps. The timestamps can be seen as the beginning and ending of a scene held within a film strip. This section of the film strip is what they call an Era upon the

Earthly Worlds. While the movements of those images held within, are simply motions towards the past or the future.

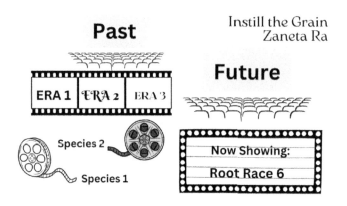

When it comes to the Universal structure *(both form and formless)* it has its own intelligence. This intelligence is seen in the form of a sphere *(1)* that surrounds these worlds. Inside of that sphere is another sphere *(2)* which is the essence of the intelligence. Inside of that sphere is yet another sphere *(3)* which the Earthly Worlds reside. It is from this blueprint that the human was mirrored. Then there is the Soul created by the gods with an immortal seed planted by THE GOD. Then they created a mortal form which is the human body. Next, they created an essence that is the messenger between the two forms, that of the immortal and the mortal. This essence is seen in the

New Age Community as the *Higher Self* aspect. This is where you have the trinity.

*Mušhuššu on a vase of Gudea, circa 2000 BC,* {{PD-US}}

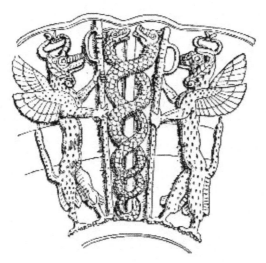

*1910 drawing of the vase,* {{PD-US}}

# Center of the Universe: God Portal
## Instill the Grain
### Zaneta Ra

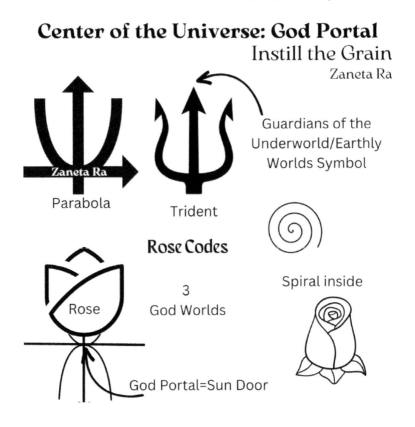

Parabola

Trident

Guardians of the Underworld/Earthly Worlds Symbol

**Rose Codes**

Rose

3
God Worlds

Spiral inside

God Portal=Sun Door

The trinity is also seen in the emblem of a Trident. The trident is seen in paintings of the gods *(Ex: Shiva and Neptune)* who oversee the God Portal Gateway. This is known in legends as The Sun Door and typically portrayed surrounded by two Sphinx *(Cherubim)* or two serpents. This doorway is in the center of the Universe and can be related as a parabola. When you look upon the previous image, you can clearly see how it appears as a trident. This symbol is layered with

46

meaning, for it also can be seen as the doorway surrounded by the two guardians.

# Meri: Christos

As taught in our book *Rising Merits*, Meri means *pearl* and is a representation of your Soul. From this ancient teaching arose the teachings of the Rose Codes. When you look upon the previous image, you can see the trice-tipped rose as a representation of the God Worlds. The reason it is seen here with three tips is because there are three God Worlds, as well as the three aspects of yourself previously mentioned.

The way creation of man was taught in the ancient temples was through the metaphors of a garden, seed, and a rose *(also seen as a lily or a lotus)*. As previously stated, it was from the gods that the human was molded. This is the rose planted in the garden. The seed is what was implanted by THE GOD SOURCE blessed with immortality, this is the Christos Seed. When a seed of man is planted into the womb, is it not the woman who nurtures it as it forms?

The spiral of life is seen as the pregnancy term of the human form laced as those magical film *(timestamps)* strips. The garden is none other than the Universe of form. When the seed has grown and is ready to be harvested, it passes through the God Portal into the worlds of formless. This route can be seen as the expansion of the seed of a rose. It forms a stem, then the bud itself.

*Statuette figure of a goddess with a horned headdress, possibly Ishtar, Astarte or Nanaya, 3rd century BC- 3rd century AD, Louvre Museum, {{PD-US}}*

When it comes to Mortal Worlds, they are the garden, and the garden is the feminine principle. This garden is known in its wholeness as the goddess Gaia/Gaea in Greek Mythology. The goddesses seen with the crescent shape is not the metaphor of the Moon, it is the parabola, the God Portal. The body of the feminine is represented as the Universe of form. The crown of the head represents the top of this universal form. The crown also is the center of this universal form where the entrance into the God Worlds resides. The seeds of the gods, meaning the man race, is nurtured within the womb of this universal form. When it comes to the Moon, is it not when its full that we hardness its energy? Now, think why would we display it when its energy is not in its entirety.

The letter E in the ancient temples denoted a temple itself *(seen carved in some ancient temples still standing)*. The word Ain was the original form of what is called Eden today, meaning we called it E-Ain. Ain in the original tongue means *one* or *woman*. The macro meaning of the original teachings of the virgin Meri implanted with the immortal Christ Seed, is from the creation of the humans and the Earthly Worlds. The meaning of being a virgin was not as it means today. In the ancient days we taught it as being bare, as in without a garden and seeds. The wholeness of the Christos Seed is the man race which expands outside of this Earthly plane.

There are many rows in a garden and each with a multitude of seeds. The seeds in a single row represent

49

a film reel, meaning a specific man species. The next row represents another Earthly World with another man species *(Ex: Pleiades, Andromeda etc.)* and so forth. When the seeds are ready for harvest, they ascend from the Earth and into the Air. Do you see the representation of the depths in which we speak. The teachings of the Trident and the Rose have been lost due to man using the mortal mind to decode. If one stills the mortal mind and simply observes nature itself, then one will gain all the keycodes.

# Axis Mundi

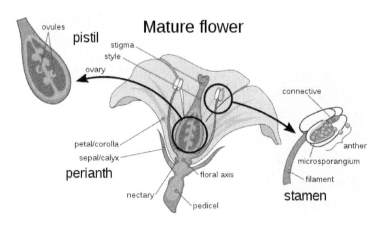

*Main parts of a mature flower, Mariana Ruiz,* {{PD-US}}

In the previous image, when you look at the sepal you can see the same shape as the parabola and the crescent. Just above that is where the nectar resides. In

50

the sacred teachings of climbing the 33 steps of Jacobs ladder, at the top is where the lamp oil is lit. This is related to where the nectar *(oil)* resides, which is accessed via the 33 vertebrae of the human spine.

---

*"Blood stem cells are formed in red bone marrow. Most red bone marrow is housed in the vertebrae. Once the stem cells are formed, they go into the thymus gland to become T cells. These are the white blood cells that house your DNA. As the Higher crystal heart is forming (via the CHRISTOS blueprint anchoring) in the thymus, it is completely shifting the DNA formation of the T cells."*

*~Cracking the Chrysalis: Shattering the Steps of Ascension*

---

The Soul is able to inhabit the human form through the spine which can be seen as the stem of the flower. It can drip the sacred honey *(nectar)* from the crown to the incarnate *(seed)*. This sacred flow is seen as a serpent and is the pure representation of wisdom because that is what your Soul was molded from.

The spine can also be seen as the trunk of a tree. The roots are grounded into the soil, Earth, where the branches expand upward into the God Worlds, Air. This is where the legends of the World Tree stem from. The World spoken of in the ancient temples were about the entire Mortal World. We called this the Axis Mundi which is known today as the *naval of the world.*

*Caduceus*

It is at the naval, the center of the Universe of form, that you will find the God Portal. As stated previously, it is always seen with two guardians.

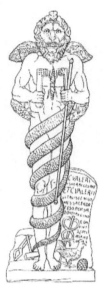

*Drawing of the lion-headed figure found at the Mithraeum of C. Valerius Heracles and sons, dedicated 190 CE at Ostia Antica, Italy,* {{PD-US}}

The combination of man laced in a serpent, holding keys, and with wings, is the trinity of the divine inheritance you all have.

This was seen in Ancient Egypt as the Solar Gateway. When you see the god Osiris, he is adorned with a crown that resembles the pistil and the stamen of a mature flower. He is also seen as green, just like mother nature. As taught in the Rising Merits book, this merely was the representation of your Christos. It is only through the Christos can one fly into the Sun and merge as one again with their Higher Self.

*Osiris, tomb QV66,* {{PD-US}}

The goddess Isis is seen as the Higher Self, which is the mother aspect our incarnate self was birthed from. The winged Sun is her symbol to represent the famous God Portal we speak of. The next image is of Nefertari. As you see the codes layered in her crown. You clearly see the Solar disc with the two pillars, the God Portal. Which is seated atop a bird. The bird, which is an emblem of Gaia herself, the Universe of Form, the Mortal Worlds *(For a deeper understanding of the Pearl Teachings from Ancient Egypt please reference the **Rising Merits** book).*

*Nefertari, circa 1298-1235 BCE, US-PD*

# God Worlds

The God Worlds exist within the Universe of Formless. It is within this formless universe that the legends of the three heavens stem. When God Source created the gods, they wished for their own Garden to plant seeds of their own and to create. When this was requested, God Source stated that the Universe of Form and Formless were to be created at the same time. If the Universe of Form was to destroy itself, so too would the Universe of Formless. This first creation is known as the gods Uranus and Gaia, which represent Tier I of the God Worlds.

In our commandments taught in the *Angelic Pearls 144* book, we taught of the meaning of an orange. Oranges are seen in the garden along with the gods to denote life itself for the mortals. You have the orange in its wholeness, yet you also have the segments within it. It was from the orange of Uranus and Gaia that the 12 gods of Tier II were segmented.

It is from their seeds that make up Tier III. It is from this world that the elements and all of the material forms were crafted. The gods of Tier III truly are the artisans of all that exists within the Universe of form. As you study the diagram of the 3 God Worlds, you will notice how each of their seeds oversee each element. For example, the seeds of Iapetus oversee the element fire. When we speak of fire, one must grasp what this truly means in every aspect. Fire can be seen as a flame, embers of a fire as well as a burning flame.

Another example, you have the seeds of Oceanus that oversee the element water. When it comes to water it can be liquid or more solid. Meaning it can be made into more dense uniformed particles or composed of smaller ununiformed particles.

# 3 God Worlds

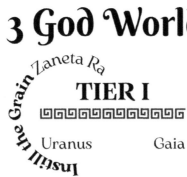

## TIER I

Uranus          Gaia

## TIER II

Oceanus +     Hyperion +   Mnemosyne +   Coeus +
Tethys          Theia          Themis          Phoebe

Cronus +                          Crius +
Rhea                              Iapetus

## TIER III

Seeds of     Seeds of     Seeds of     Seeds of     Seeds of
Crius        Oceanus      Hyperion     Coeus        Iapetus

Seeds of
Cronus

I=Mother + Father Aspects
II=Their 12 Aspects
III=Their seeds which oversee the Universe of Form

# Tier 111

## 🔲🔲🔲🔲🔲🔲🔲🔲🔲
## Instill the Grain

### Zaneta Ra

**Seeds of Crius**

- Persus
- Pallas
- Astraeus

*Overseers of Air*

**Seeds of Oceanus**

- Oceanids
- Potamoi

*Overseers of Water*

**Seeds of Hyperion**

- Helios
- Selene
- Eos

*Overseers of Ether*

**Seeds of Coeus**

- Leto
- Asteria

*Overseers of Earth*

**Seeds of Iapetus**

- Atlas
- Prometheus
- Menoetius
- Epimetheus

*Overseers of Fire*

**Seeds of Cronus**

- Zeus
- Hera
- Hades
- Poseid
- Hestia
- Damator *(Demeter)*
- Karren *(Chiron)*
- Typhon
- Corybantes

*Overseers of the Blueprints/Garden/ Timekeepers*

# Seeds of Cronus

When it comes to the seeds of Cronus, they are most known in Greek Mythology as the famous Zeus, Hades, Poseidon etc. There are nine all together that oversee the material garden. Meaning that they make sure the Divine Blueprints approved by God Source is aligned. This is time itself or what is labelled as timelines.

When it came to the material garden being created, God Source stated to implant into it the immortal seed which is known today as the Christ Seed. This seed was implanted into all creations of the Universe of Form. However, the macro seed is the seed of the universe body itself which is seen as the metaphor of the goddess Gaia, *(as we mentioned in the previous chapter)*.

The reason that the nature of the name Cronus is time is because that is existence of the mortal essence. The nine aspects of Cronus created the mortal form. Zeus was known by the nature of the names Zena and Dia *(spoken of in Plato's work Cratylus)* prior to the times of antiquity. This is where the origin of the word zen *(lifeforce)* stems from. Zeus simply emitted the creation of the essence known as Light or the Christos. Hades emitted the nature of the shadows. Here is where all mortals have the essences of both chaos and love, meaning, light and dark. It is about learning how to balance them both that makes one a master.

## Seeds of Cronus
### Instill the Grain
### Zaneta Ra

- **Hestia**=Fire/Breath
- **Zeus**=Light/Christos
- **Hades**=Shadow/Mirror
- **Damator**=Grain/Higher Self
- **Poseid**=Water/Plasma Body
- **Hera**=Time/Mortal Existence
- **Karren**=Vessel/Body
- **Typhon**=Head/Mind
- **Corybantes**=Peak/Crown: essence communication tower

*They are formless and merely represent an elixir that of form seeded from.*

It is from their own elixirs that the Man race was crafted. Let us break them down a little more:

**Hestia:** Gave breath to the mortal

**Zeus:** Gave the Christ light to the mortal

**Hades:** Gave the reflection known as shadow to the mortal

**Damator:** Gave the elixir of the Higher Self to the mortal

**Poseid:** Gave the Plasma/Light body to the mortal

**Hera:** Gave a lifetime/incarnation itself to the mortal

**Karren:** Gave a vessel for the immortal essence known as a mortal body

**Typhon:** Gave the mind/intelligence to the mortal

**Corybantes:** Gave the Crown Chakra, which is how the intelligence can communicate to the mortal form

# Seeds of Mnemosyne

When it comes to the seeds of Mnemosyne, they reside outside of time itself because they represent it. Meaning they reside outside of the Universe of Form as well as outside of the Universe of Formless. The term hourglass stems from Horae as well as the god Horus, whose nature simply represents a time portal. When it comes to this local Sun System, the hours are seen in the original 12 planetary bodies. We call them spheres of time with each vibrating at a different speed. Remember, time was created to compartmentalize the mortal existence. The seeds of Mnemosyne assisted with this creation.

# Seeds of Mnemosyne
## Instill the Grain
## Zaneta Ra

## Muses

9 Ego layers of the
mind=your reality

## Moirai

*Fate*
They oversee the
destiny of all
Mortals

## Horae

*Hours*
They oversee the hours
held within each Timeline

- *12 original planets=spheres of TIME*
- *12-hour marks of the Sun Time*
- *12 Positive=Day Time*
- *12 Negative=Night Time*

The Muses are seen as nine to represent the nine ego layers of the mortal mind which simply is a micro reflection to the Astral Body. Sometimes the Muses are seen as three because they are this as well. What we mean is they represent the 3x3 equation, representing that of light, shadow, and a balance. These can be seen as the meninges that envelop the spinal cord and the brain. The three meninges are the arachnoid matter *(light Muse)*, dura matter *(shadow Muse)*, and the pia mater *(Muse of unity)*.

The ego itself is not fully visible but houses the elixirs of those mentioned membranes. They reside within your Physical Body, Emotional Body, and your Mental Body. Three within each is how you get the total of nine Muses. It is the combination of them all that creates your own reality.

---

*"Next to the Emotional Body is the Mental Body. The way you feel is created by your Mental Body because it is fed by your Emotional Body. This is where the saying "mind over matter" comes into play. The matter represents your Physical Body where the mind references your Mental Body. Think of your Emotional Body like a paint palette in your hand. Each paint color is a different vibrational frequency representing your emotions. The paint brush represents your Mental Body. These tools work together to paint your reality upon the canvas. Each hue of color on the canvas is a match to the mixture you selected. In other words, the vibrations you emit is what helps to paint your reality."*

## ~Cracking the Chrysalis: Shattering the Steps of Ascension

The balance of these three bodies is very important to your vibrational field. The Universe itself is a sphere within a sphere, within another sphere. It too houses these bodies and must stay balanced to carry out the Divine Blueprint. When you allow your emotions to control you it alters your destiny, your path in this lifetime. If one was to think positively then it sends out those higher vibrations and boomerangs back into your field that of a like vibration. This is what the Muses do. This is what we teach as the Laws of Action. For it is the action of your own vibrations that craft what you "see" around you.

The seeds of Mnemosyne are the nature of the Metatronic Mind. The 12 aspects are seen as each creation within the Universe Form. Meaning that of a Sun System as well as the mortal essence themselves. This is where you have the codex known today as the flower of life. You can see held within the flower of life symbol the Metatron's Cube, which is denoted in the next diagram image. Each planetary body can be seen as each of the 12 circles. The center sphere can be seen as the Sun that birthed the 12 bodies, just like your Higher Self as well as the gods Uranos and Gaia.

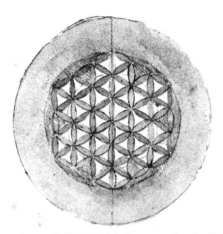

*Codex Atlanticus, 1478-1519, Leonardo da Vinci,* {{PD-US}}

*Mosaic floor from a bathhouse in Herod's palace, 1st century BCE,* {{PD-US}}

When ancients spoke of the other planetary bodies, in truth they speak of a vibration. The reality you exist in is crafted by yourself. Yes, you are birthed within a specific density but then you are given the tools to ascend to higher vibrational planes. The teachings taught in the ancient Temples were about this. They taught of the marga path which has been translated today as *"the way"*. Marga in ancient Greek simply means pearl. Marga is still seen today in ancient Sanskrit as a pathway to spiritual awakening because it is only through your light, your pearl-essence can you ascend. There is no other way.

*Mnemosyne, Dante Gabriel Rossetti, between 1876-1881,*
{{PD-US}}

# The Astral Plane

The nature of the nine Muses makes up what is best known today as the Astral World or the Astral Plane. When it comes to the existence of the Astral, it resides from the Macro to the Micro. This means that you not only have this field around the body of Earth, but around the entire Universe of form, which simply houses the Earthly Worlds.

The Astral houses all that emits as a thought from not only the mortal mind but also that of the Emotional Body and Mental Body. The result that is emitted from the mortal mind is crafted by these other two bodies. Taken what we previously taught of the Muses being that of light, shadow, or unity; the equation of them all equals the reality presented. Therefore, this can be a matrix birthed out of the shadows, light, or of unification of energies.

Once one is no longer operated by the mortal mind, it becomes fully operated by the essence of its Light which resides in the Universe of Formless. This is when one has truly become unified with their Higher Self and has started their transformation into a formless being.

# Astral Particles

The mind of a Light Master is quiet because his consciousness field is no longer one with that of the Earth Plane. Meaning that he is no longer fed thoughts from the collective consciousness, which is the Mental Body of Earth. The Mental Body of Earth is directly linked with your own, like an infinity symbol.

These very thoughts are the particles of Souls once incarnated here. They are fragmented portions of the Emotional and Mental Bodies of those Souls that became stuck within the Astral Plane at the time of death. It also is a place where all thoughts, ideas, and beliefs of man reside. The Astral Plane is a polarity field because it houses both positive and negative particles.

The very thoughts that enter the mind of someone on their path are these particles. It is only when the person chooses to feed energy to a particle does it start to grow and if it is fed enough energy then it can become propelled to take on a form. When it comes to negative energy, the Higher Light Arks give them a choice to either come to the light side or become fragmented into the elements of Earth. It is these same larger negative entities that can consume someone who is primarily of the light.

When it comes to part of the original Ascension plans to rescue the stuck particles of light, it was to send in higher fields of consciousness that can hear these particles. Most of the time they either stem from a fragmented aspect of that Soul or they are of another Light Master that came prior. When you hear a thought and you choose to feed it energy by turning it into something more concrete, if it is for the highest good of humanity then you help to release it. It is no longer bound to the Astral. The same works for the negative thought particles.

When one tries to connect to a higher field, what they are doing is plugging into the Astral Plane. This is where the release of such a force of negative energies started. These very energies can consume a human vessel to the point of a full possession. However, if you continue to actively connect solely with your own Spirit, then you will become possessed by it and this is the moment when your flesh turns into light. Each time you tune into your light and breathe it into your form, it anchors into your cells. Ascension happens when those very cells can no longer hold any more light and completely transform. You then shift and become one with your light.

The Muses portrayed in legends are placing men into a trance state can now be decoded as this. When it comes to thoughts of mortals, they are seen no different than that of God Source. All of Creation is simply a thought. However, each thought can house within it a Light Seed or a Dark Seed. If you have a seed in a garden that becomes tainted, it can spread to the rest of the garden. So too can the Light Seeds. The Light Seeds are the purest form of the elixirs created by the gods. It was only those particles of dark that overtime stripped some of the seeds from the light.

Since all is connected, if the seeds all become impure, what do you think will occur in the God Worlds. We gifted our creation with the freedom to create upon themselves, however, a time has come where a portion of the garden is becoming untended. It is that of which we sent out the purest forms of ourselves to help instill the grain. Meaning, we sent out our sacred gold dust to help pollenate the untended garden. We call to you now, to remember.

*"To the elect incarnated, this gold dust is held in their energetic field. It filters into the energetic field of an initiate upon interaction. The golden dust is seeded and fed light by their own Christos self. It will then ignite into their physical DNA causing upgrades and activations. This is how sacred sigils and symbols work, connecting those of the physical planes to the higher planes of light. The key is to look upon them using your heart crystal, allowing that diamond light cord within to connect you to your higher crystal heart."*

**~Angelic Pearls 144**, *Gold Dust chapter*

# Zodi Act

The knowledge of Astrology and the Zodiac Wheel is not taught in its original state as we did in the ancient temples. The term Zodi speaks of the dust emitted from the Sun. Zodi dust is the gold dust used throughout this Universe to create material forms. The body of the man race was created by this dust. This dust is a combination of all the material elements and thus for, all lifeforms are sustained by it. It is the golden dust that pollinates the garden.

The ancient teachings that the Sun provides life, holds more depth than one can grasp. As we taught in the book *Angelic Pearls 144,* this Universe consists of 144 Suns that are fed directly from Source. The totality of those Suns is the Universal Christ Seed. It feeds this light into the smaller galactic Suns that then create

Zodi for its world systems. Zodi is the densified form of heavenly honey sent from the Worlds of Light.

The famous Phaistos Disc is very similar to how we used the original Zodi Wheel. We brought to Earth a disc with 13 sections. This teaching disc was used to show the cycle of life for this Universe. It explains the ascension and descension of the Zodi.

# Zodic Act: Light Seed to Man

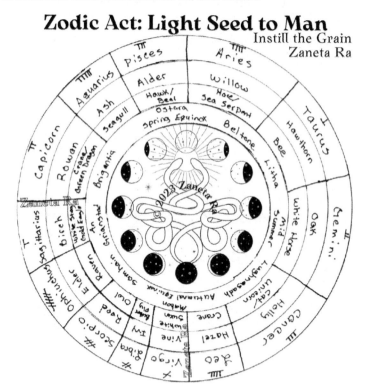

*Wheel created by Zaneta Ra, ©2023 Zaneta Ra*

There is much hidden and kept from humanity over the last 8,000 linear years. We laugh at the way humans believe a sign determines their personality when this cannot be further from the truth. What each segment holds are an energetic impression of the life cycle.

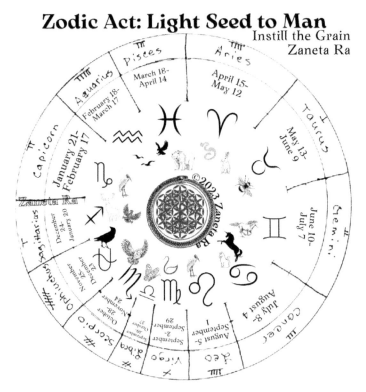

*Wheel created by Zaneta Ra, ©2023 Zaneta Ra*

The sign **Aquarius** symbolizes THE MIND, the Creator, the Cosmic Waters, the very fountain of existence. It is from here that the thought of THE MIND *(Pisces)* created Divine Will *(Aries/Ares/Kres/Crete)*. The Divine Will is the wish, the very thought projected out from the Creator. One of those thought forms is the Man Race.

As above, so below. Since everything stems from THE MIND, a micro version needed to be created. Therefore, before the Man Race could come into form, the mind *(Taurus/Tortoise)* was created. The shell of a tortoise holds the body, a lifeform, an essence. This is your Crown, the very location where the Divine Masculine and Divine Feminine energies flow *(Gemini)* into the mortal form.

Next, we created the Emotional Body *(Cancer)*. Then we created the Mental Body *(Leo)*. We then needed to create a pure form for Spirit to travel existence with, so we created the Light Body *(Virgo)*. We then needed to create a form for Spirit to travel within the Worlds of Form, so we created the Physical Body *(Libra)*. To bring these bodies into motion, we sent the serpent fire *(Scorpio)* into them, we gave them life. However, we also knew that these forms would need a messenger from the Higher Planes where their full consciousness exists and to the dense bodies. We needed to create serpent barriers *(Ophiuchus)* that bring life, the pure Christos to these bodies. We then needed to protect this energy and who gains access to this so it does not overload the dense bodies, so we created Archers/Guardians *(Sagittarius)*. This essence holds guard over the serpent breath, the Divine Wisdom.

When these codes are ready to be received into the body of form, it is gifted into the Divine Crown *(Capricorn)*. The sacred golden honey is poured into the body via this sacred river. The sacred river that connects the Worlds of Seen and the Worlds of the Unseen.

# Energy Act

Each segment upon the Zodi wheel holds an action, an essence of existence for the mortal man. When it comes to the segment known as Libra, this is associated with the measurement of mass, meaning density. The symbol for this denotes the butterfly which signifies transformation. On the Zodi wheel you will notice it is seen as Ivy. Ivy continues to grow and can take over buildings created by man. Ivy is seen as the flow of eternity.

The goal of man is to transform the flesh just how a caterpillar does. To seek transfiguration from the chrysalis as a butterfly. This is why in ancient Egypt the god Osiris was connected to ivy. Learning in *Rising Merits* that Osiris symbolizes your Christos Body, you can see now why ivy and Libra also depict this sacred teaching.

The essence of the Light Body that is used in the stage of transfiguration is seen as the white swan. The purity of a swan is denoted by the segment Virgo. The original teachings that your incarnate self are the branches, and your god self is the vine simply signifies how you descended from your Higher essence. The very pure pearl-essence that is your virgin self, your Light Body.

Another famous symbol is the white stag. The stag is seen with our beautiful Artemis and is denoted with the Sagittarius segment. This is the protector, the guardian of the sacred garden. This is where the legends of Artemis as a hunter was misconstrued, for she is the protector. The stag eats of the fruit of the garden. The very essence within you that craves to eat from the sacred guardian can be seen as the white stag *(As seen in the next image with the Christos upon the stag)*.

*13ᵗʰ Century illuminated manuscript depicting St Eustace
and the white hart* {{PD-US}}

The Zodi Act simply is a sacred teaching wheel to present mankind with a play of their lifecycle. Each segment merely is an act played upon the stage of life. Everyone plays a part that is known as an archetype. Examples are those who play the:

- Wise One
- Warrior
- Seeker
- Ruler
- Magician
- Fool
- Destroyer and many more

It is only when you retract from the stage and simply observe it will you truly understand it. This is when you come into a state of neutrality. This is when you gain enlightenment.

# Zodi Act Symbols

Instill the Grain
Zaneta Ra

 Light Body=Virgin
essence

 Physical Body=
Transformation

 Serpent Breath=
Life

 Serpent Barrier=Divine
Messenger (Oracle)

 Archer/Guardian

# Zodi Act Symbols

Instill the Grain
Zaneta Ra

Gold Dust/Christos

Cosmic Waters/Fountain of Existence

Thought of THE MIND/Creator

Divine Will= Sword

Mind Shell

Masculine: Feminine essence

Emotional Body

Mental Body

# Hammer of the Gods

*Zaneta Ra:* When I read Timaeus by Plato, I was not happy to see the end where Zeus was to speak was conveniently "lost". The dialogue was about how the seeds were becoming impure and Zeus was not happy, therefore, he held a council with the other gods. He goes to speak, and the book just ends. I was curious, what did he say?

Since I have always spoke with the Angels, I was flabbergasted to see the ceiling of my bedroom open and the bottom of two ginormous sandals appear. As the figure slowly emerged, I noticed it was no other than Zeus himself. I am then taken to appear before him in his world. The first words I hear telepathically are *abomination to antiquity.* I then asked Zeus:

*"What did you command in that moment?"*

*Zeus:* Implement the Divine Codex. Treaty of defilement and abomination. Infirmament the seas and land by which thou inherited through Divine Will and Testament of my essence. The very essence your seeded intelligence was crafted. The essence sowed into thee with Divine instructions to cherish and tend. Through self-serving actions and powers of greed, thee has broken. 12,000 years, an era in time, was gifted to reform from disciplinary actions by which the moment of servitude has now enveloped.

*Zaneta Ra:* What he is speaking about is the distortion of the man race around the year 9977 BC. What I was shown was several thousand years prior to that time, man drifted away from the Divine Laws place before them. It is a time where the evolution of Atlantis formed. This is an energy field that was fed through a portal from timelines of the last 20,000 plus years. Atlantis itself exist in the future of this time node due to the defilement Zeus speaks of. The 12,000 years is a time where man was gifted to either reform from those actions or continue to defile the Divine Laws once taught. This is where the separation of timelines and fields of consciousness are slowly occurring as we speak. The times of antiquity were from around 8,000 BC to 5th Century AD. He references that a time has come where those tainted seeds in the garden must be separated from the rest of the garden because they can no longer be saved. The rest of the message is layered for those to decipher as their essence deems so. The rest of the dialogue is from this now moment for the purpose of this book.

*"Please elaborate on the nature of names, specifically yours."*

**Zeus:** The nature of all things both known and unknown, were once provided a natural label, which has sense been lost due to the times of antiquity. I am known as that spoken of as Zeus, Zen, Odin, Amun-Ra, Dagda, Michael, and many more. Each hold within them the same nature as the other yet understood as a truth to the seeker that uses that implication. If you take your name Zaneta, it was provided using the nature of the Hebrew tongue, yet it is Ioannes in ancient Greek, however, through other implications it is Yohan, John, Joan, and Johannes. Even though when you were born it was under the truth that it was from the Hebrew tongue, yet now as I have disclosed it is seen as other truths among other tongues spoken. What is meant here is that from one's truth a label is used yet from another's it is their truth to use a different kind of label. The labels are all defining the same nature just spoken with another truth. It has become lost over time and over many tongues and minds the full understandings of this teaching. The reason this occurs was to provide that from each standpoint is a nature that aligns with one of the rays of Creation, which within itself houses its own vibration. It too is also one in the same with another ray of Creation, and another, and another, then all together as the mighty pearl. What we taught in the lands of our offspring was to understand all views and angles of the many eyes of Creation. To understand that within your wholeness houses many other natures.

Another lesson upon this lecture I speak is that from the ancient name of Zaneta you have the English name John. Looking upon the two one would never assume such. This is the lesson of how far off a small stream of water has wandered from the Ocean. One example I shall use that has traveled far from Athena's teachings is that of the word demon. This original nature is that of *daemon (soter/daimon)* which denotes an all-powerful, protective yet wise god. Due to the nature, it is now being presented to many as that of the opposite. When you diversify the nature of existence by using many labels, what one is truly doing is defiling the pure essence of its core nature. This is where coming back to feeling that which is, instead of trying to decipher that which is not, needs to arise within the teachings of enlightenment sought out upon the mortal worlds.

*"Are there any more words of wisdom you wish to express at this now time?"*

*Zeus:* It is that of which is unseen that transforms that which is seen. Seeds are all planted from a thought. As they are given attention they tend to grow. Yet gardens grow overnight from a feeling. A simple feeling from the combination of your essence that is both seen, and unseen can transform the entire existence you reside within. Time is a sphere, and you are encased within it. If you walk forward, the sphere moves with you. If you walk backwards, the sphere moves with you. You control the sphere; the sphere does not control you.

# Thor

*"What does the hammer represent?"*

*Tor:* The hammer denotes the Divine Law and Protection between that of the seen and unseen worlds. My original symbol is seen as such with the two crossing. This emblem has a layered meaning. It is the pure flow of the seen and unseen together as one. Where they meet denotes a doorway. I am the protector who oversees this doorway. This is the doorway of the essence of the Divine Law of the gods. I do not physically hold a hammer; it is merely a representation of the throw down of the Divine Law if it is not obeyed upon the worlds beneath that of the gods. I am the protector of the pure. I am seen as a protector over those who obey the Divine Will as written in the Book of Life. Those who do not obey this fall upon the incarnation cycle, unable to walk past the doorway of which I am and into the world of the unseen. This is none other than the Sun Door spoken of throughout the realms of the mortals.

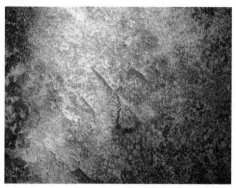

*Swastika on the Snoldelev stone 9th century AD, in the National Museum of Copenhagen, Denmark,*

**"Can you speak on your Egyptian aspect?"**

*Tor:* I am that which is known as Ptah and the djed is the hammer. I am known as the god of forge and fire and therefore known to the ancient lands around the central sea *(he speaks of the Mediterranean)* as the god Hephaestus. It was during this time when wars were

89

raging among the central sea that I taught man how to forge weaponry. I taught them in ways of protection. In the lands of Egypt, I taught this as well however, the weaponry was that of the spirit. The djed hammer resides as the style in a flower. It is what protects the pocket where the nectar is nurtured. I am that who protects the nectar located within the worlds of the unseen. The very elixir that the essence from the world of seen fermented.

*"Do you have anything else you wish to speak of?"*

*Tor:* I wish to speak of the ravens. As the seeds of us wandered further from the Ocean as Zeus spoke of, we were no longer able to walk the lands of the seen. Many statues of the gods, the eyes were hexed to keep us from seeing inside of the seen world. We work with the birds to see through their eyes. Raven was once spoken of as fiach/fiak which is where the denotation of fairies' stem from. This is because they are one in the same, for we work with them both. They are the messengers able to traverse both the seen and unseen. It was during the times of antiquity that we sent Oracles. For not only are we able to speak through them, but we can also see through their eyes as well. Oracles, birds such as ravens and owls, and fairies are always associated together for this reason. They are all our messengers. They are all our seers.

*Greek Keys as depicted in Ottův slovník naučný, 1900,*
{{PD-US}}

*Zaneta Ra:* In the Greek Keys image you can clearly see the symbol Tor spoke of which is known as the swastika. Going back to what the 144 spoke of about the God Portal surrounded by two serpents, you can clearly see it symbolized here. We find these symbols in so many ancient artifacts. I have seen images of ancient Nordic swords with this symbol on them as well as many ancient ruins. We see this linked in the ancient Celts artifacts as well.

To make note of the word *infirmament* Zeus used, I can explain the visons he provided me along with that message. What he means is to make weak, to turn that which is pure into unclean lands and waters. I clearly asked to make sure he did not mean the biblical term firmament. He made it clear *infirmament* is an archaic expression.

I would lastly like to make note that in ancient Greece it was a custom to dedicate a third wine offering to Zeus the Saviour *(Soter)*. Soter was the term he told me was used to express the "Seed". In this context it was honoring the *Christ Seed*, which when ignited does taste *(savor)* like vanilla honey in the back of your throat. Zeus was also titled "Zef" which is translated today to the name Yossef. Zef was used in the context as father *(see the understanding of father under Brigid in* **God Aspects***).*

# Goddess Artemis

The goddess Artemis is known today mostly as the mistress of the hunt or as the goddess Diana. Just like all other feminine deities, she merely represents an essence of the Divine Mother. This same essence is part of the elixir so many Soul Sparks were created from. This is why so many see Artemis as their guide at some point along their spiritual path.

The reason her essence or any others appear to individuals are because it is part of a specific initiation. Each person will have their own unique experience that is aligned for their highest good at obtaining enlightenment.

The essence of Artemis is the first to great me almost every time I enter the Emerald City of the God Kingdoms. She is not one single entity but merely a manifestation of Divine Mother. Just how the Christos Angels are a walking manifestation of The Sun sent here to reflect light onto all we encounter. This Sun is the heart center of Creator also known as The Christ Seed.

When I first encountered Artemis, I had never heard of her before. She appeared to me as a beautiful celestial swan in a blue pond. She then exited the pond and slowly morphed into a beautiful goddess. She said she was *Artemis of the Paramahamsas*. She informed me that the meaning of Paramahamsa is a title of an enlightened Light Master. The meaning of the celestial swan symbolizes purity and that of royalty. The swan atop the blue waters symbolized her role to oversee the Cosmic Ocean. The depths of the Underworld are linked to that of an Ocean.

## Conversation with Artemis

*"What is the connection of the Greek gods to the Sphere we call Earth and to humanity which exist upon it?"*

*Artemis:* The ones of whom humanity term as "gods" existed before the creation of the physical body known as Earth. When the Solar System was created there was a council created to oversee the evolution of the physical manifestations. These physical manifestations were brought about by a higher council known as the architects of this Universe which we term "Dimension". Within this Dimension you have several planes of existence which are termed "Density".

The Mans created for this planet were originally created with a 7th plane blueprint. Throughout many experiences it was deemed best suited for this planet that we shift the Man to a 5th plane level of existence. This was due to the fact that Earth was created in this density with the plan to advance up to the 7th plane. We originally felt by Man being slightly on a higher plane it would help to smooth the shifting and enhance the living experience. Other lifeforms such as the nature kingdom were already thriving on Earth in a 5th level plane of existence.

Prior to Man coming on this planet, we had many existing within the Animal and Elemental Kingdoms. For the Elemental Kingdom was charged by Divine to be the over seers of the Nature and Animal Kingdoms *(this is where the legend of the god Pan stems from).*

When Man was created, it was learned that Man would best thrive when "born" of the elements which already existed on the planet. Each Man species we injected on this planet of existence censed to evolve. When PanGaea *(all Earth)* thrived and all were one with the planet, we also had pockets scattered around the planet where we helped teach the Man of this planet. This is the accurate timeframe when those termed as demigods were created. For some gods did mate with their very own creations. For we see all as Source and all as ONE. We do not see separation of creations but as ONE unity field of existence. This later became known as *The Laws of One.*

The next stage was to implement Spirituality into the planet and the Man. This is when the lovely Naara's *(Venusians)* from Earth's sister planet volunteered to come and set up Mother Temples. What is now known today as Lake Titicaca used to be located more closer inward of the now Pacific Ocean, this area was the Sacral Chakra of the planet and thus for known as the womb of The Mother. This was the ideal location for this Mother Temples to be birthed onto the planet.

This is where we created the first physical layers of Shamballa. For Shamballa exist on all planes of the planet. Yes, it was once physical and was the main entrance to the Temple of the Sun. Housing within it were the major deities of Love from the Planet of Love,

Venus. For this is the heart of the Solar System. From the heart lies the portal to ALL in existence.

This is what these beings came to teach as well as experience life on this newly developed and terra formed planet. Which from afar the neighboring planets have been observing with great excitement. For see at this time Venus the planet had just gone thru its very own Ascension and was eager to teach all this Divine knowledge. For many great teachers from not only this Universe but others as well come to Venus to train and learn from the Elohim of the Third Flame of the Divine All.

There once was a time of great harmony and alignment upon the planet, this is the fantasy land many within the human collective dream of. This is Utopia many remember and long to reunite with once again. This Utopia reigns on planet Venus in the Higher Planes and is designed to be once again during the Great Golden Age timeline which Earth is now aligned on.

Now, you ask what our role in humanity was? Well, it was simply this, to teach, monitor, and report. There was a time we existed with you however, on a Higher Plane. We have never truly left; we are emanated on some and guides/mentors/teachers for others. Some train with us when their vessel rests, some have even taught us. For there are many advanced Souls from 10-12th dimension upon the planet. Keep in mind pupils that the Architects of this Universe reside in the 10-12th dimension. Within each dimension there are believe it or not unlimited planes of existence. This is not something the mortal mind can comprehend for it exist outside a linear mental template.

When one connects to the 10-12th dimension, they are not connecting to just one being but to all. For they then become unified in these levels and there are no linear ways of communication. This is why learning to use one's heart and not the voice box or physical brain is the key. These beings that exist here are the ones termed as Archangels, Seraphs, The EL's, Cherubs, and the Thrones. They hold no form here. They simply just ARE and experience no separation and no suffering. They are our Creators, if you will label it this way.

These are whom we report to for they sit at the MIGHTY THRONE OF THE ALL. When it is directed by THE ALL and Mans have reached the level of spiritual oneness within their hearts, then we will appear once again before and beside you. Our so-called Legends stem from the Greeks for they are our direct ancestors, among many other tribes on the planet. When the fall of At-Lan happened, our existence was never forgotten. Poseidon is real, I am real, and Zeus is real. We simply exist on Higher Planes and invite all whose heart aligns with what they are searching for to come to us. If you venture to the depths of your Soul; there we will be. We lie within your very own photons, open the doorway which is your heart and see us standing there. Holding the golden apple of divine wisdom and the Serpent who shows you the pathway.

*"For this now time, are there any suggestions you have for humans?"*

*Artemis:* Now is a time to stay balanced and keep your vibration high. We cannot ask this enough. The miasma that has surfaced on the planet and streaming off your electrical devices are high. As well as the purging of the collective Emotional Body. Keeping your entire energy field balanced is key. All energy should flow within and without your vessels at ease.

Lots of pure water is also key. As we move closer and closer to these celestial alignments; more veils are removing and more "light" is raining down upon you. Water consumes majority of the Sphere's body as well as your own. It is a conductor, it is LIFE, and it helps activate your codes. The golden sigils which align your very bodies.

Do not be concerned on what is coming tomorrow, for in *A now moment,* tomorrow has already happened. Focus on your bodies, listen~listen~listen to them ALL *(Energy Bodies),* for they are guiding you. Follow the serpent of your divine will in the now, allow it to move freely and shed the layers of skin that no longer serves you.

Now is not the time to be concerned of the path your fellow man is on, now is the time to create the reality that aligns with your heart. We have spoken and ask ALL to LOVE YOUR TEMPLE, HONOR YOUR TEMPLE and REMEMBER your temple hears EVERYTHING."

~The Paramahamsa's of the 9th Plane

# The Blue Arrow

Artemis is almost always seen with a bow and arrow. This is because she is a guardian of a Gateway between the Earthly Words and the God Worlds. The arrow is made of etheric blue light. Christos light in the purest form is seen as electric blue. These arrows are of the purest form of the Christos and provided directly from God Source. The same can be seen as the famous lighten bolt Zeus holds or the trident of Neptune.

If a being who is not aligned to gain access tries to invade the doorway, then the arrows are used. By Divine Law the being is always given the opportunity to shift to the light or be sent directly to Source. If they choose to not shift the light, then an arrow is drawn and the moment it touches their energy field they disintegrate. Their Soul is no more, and the energy is sent to Source to be recycled for a new creation.

*Pottery plate with Artemis as the Potnia theron, Parian work, 675-600 BC. Archaeological Museum of Mykonos, by Zde, this is not endorsed*

Mainly when the Artemis aspect appears to you it is because you are associated with portal work. Sometimes she is accompanied with the goddess Freyja *(Freya)*. She works closely with Freyja because they also oversee the Valkyrie Angels.

# Valkyrie Angels

Valkyrie Angels are known to be associated with death when it is Ascension they oversee. Death itself is merely a state of transition where the spirit is no longer bound to a physical vessel. Valkyrie Angels can be seen also as Ascension Angles because they escort you through the portal system when you Ascend into the Higher Planes.

Freyja is a deity who oversees the Valkyrie Angels, and I can attest that the Archangels known as Seraphina and Rochelle oversee their own Valkyrie Angel commands as well. These Angels mainly come to the Earthly Worlds when asked by God Source at the time when the Golden Gateway to the God Worlds open *(Ascension)*.

They lead selected Souls through a portal system which is lined in a pearlescent rainbow. This is where the legends of a rainbow bridge stem from. They will then enter a bright shining city surrounded by glowing blue water that is guarded by a giant gold serpent. Before them will appear a giant crystal castle that they will enter. They will then be escorted to stand before nine giant beings of pure light. The next steps differ for everyone.

Serpents are associated with Ascension because it signifies the rise of the Kundalini. That hot Christos fire that ignites up the spine to light the lamp which is the Crown Chakra. The serpent is coiled at the base of the spine waiting for the proper vibrational octave to ignite and allow it to appear.

When it appears, it then sheds the skin of old to be reborn anew. In that very moment it becomes enlightened and crowned. The serpent is also seen as a guardian of Divine Wisdom. If one follows it, it will guide you to the land of the golden apples. These apples merely symbolize eating of the Christos light/Light Codes. It also can be seen as retrieving a golden egg or a divine orb *(See the **Oracles** Chapter for more info)*.

*The Ash Yggdrasil, 1886, Asgard and the gods by Wägner, Wilhelm*

# Hekata

The goddess Hekata is known today by the names Hecate or Hekate. When I first met this deity, I greeted

104

her as Hekata *(He Ka Ta)*. She is known as the night aspect of the goddess Artemis. In legends she is seen with a key and snakes. She is also associated with magic and crossroads. In some writings she is spoken of as the Soteira and Mother of Angels.

Hekata is a Priestess that presides over a Gateway between this world and the God Worlds. She is a gatekeeper like Artemis as well as a Keyholder for one of the Ascension gates. This is what the key symbolizes. It is a Hekata Priestess that holds access to the Solar Gateway. Therefore, she is also associated with the Sun goddess Arinna in Hittite mythology.

The Strophalos is seen as the wheel of Hekata. It is a wheel that symbolizes a portal or a doorway. This emblem originated because she was known as the Gatekeeper that kept negative spirits out. She is known to be associated with storm gods because they are who seal the doorways. That is why for the god Thor his original symbol was a swastika. This is one of the most ancient symbols found on artifacts because it is used as protection when left faced. This was used to close a doorway where the wheel of Hekata was used to protect it. Thor and all other storm gods were seen with a hammer because they used that to seal the door.

Hekata is merely a title of a Priestess who holds these duties. One famous story of someone taken by Artemis for this sacred initiation was Iphigenia. She was the daughter of Agamemnon whose brother was married to the famous Helen of Troy. Few legends speak of her being "sacrificed" to Artemis. This word stems from "sacer" which means *sacred*. It also is connected to the word "sacart" which meant *Priest or Priestess* in the ancient tongue. This story was originally about how Iphigenia was divinely initiated as a Priestess of Artemis. However, once again we see how this has become misconstrued throughout history.

This is the same with the original teachings in the sacred temples and why going within is how you truly gain clarity and understanding. Teachings of ancient past have taken on a completely new meaning that has pushed people in seeking with their minds and not their hearts. Ancient texts and teachings are so deeply coded that if you read them for a surface level understanding, you will never gain access to their codes.

*Venus Verticordia by Dante Gabriel Rossetti, between 1864-1868, no changes made*

***Zaneta Ra:*** This painting can be seen as a symbolism of the archer protecting the sacred orange. The very fruit of the garden that symbolizes immortality. The butterflies can be seen to denote the transformation out of the flesh and into the immortal form. The very transition out of the Worlds of the Seen and into the Worlds of the Unseen, the God Worlds.

107

# The Amazons

The warrior women known today as the Amazons go back to the Solar Tribes. These are the tribes that came through the Sun, from the God Worlds to help raise the collective consciousness. We learn in the *Angelic Pearls 144* book:

*"Those of the Za Na Ta and Ma Za Ur tribe became known as the Berbers who resided in North Africa. Most who stem from this tribe reside in Morocco, Algeria, and France today. The legends of the Amazons stem from these tribes. This contributed to why in history the Berbers originally were called Amazigh. The earliest tribes in ancient Egypt were of theses tribes for they were directly*

*seeded from Lord of Venus, Zanat. The famous Zanata Stone near the Montaña de las Flores is connected to the Za Na Ta tribe. The tribe today is known as the Zenata and the famous Guanche statues are true to the forms of this sacred tribe."*

{{PD-US}} *First picture of the Berber found in the tomb of Seit I, 1820, drawing by Heinrich Menu von Minutoli*

There were 12 Tribes that came here to assist in advancing the DNA. There were advanced crystal cities in the sky they resided upon. They would take initiates to these cities for training. There were many sacred Temples there that are known today as Mystery Schools, they still exist but few are allowed access. The reason few are allowed access is due to the condition of their Emotional Body. You see, when you go to another realm, your energy field directly connects to theirs. Therefore, to learn from the Masters, you must first align your own energy field.

The Amazons were all females who sacrificed themselves to come to Earth and mate with selected humans. This was a way to help advance the DNA *(for more information see the **Angelic Pearls 144** book)*. They originally were called the Mazurs. The Guanches mentioned prior are some of their descendants.

Upon the original Mazurs you had:

10 Queens
2 Valkyrie Queens
12 Valkyries
3 Priestesses of Time/Fate
4 Archers
3 Pegasus Masters
10 Guards
21 Warriors

The reason we say original Mazurs is because these were the first ones to come to this plane. They were the ones that held 100% organic DNA from the God Planes. There came a time when men of Earth wanted to bed these women for reasons well known. It is because of this threat so-to-speak, that they became known in legends as warriors. It is true that in the beginning they would send the son's born to the Earth plane and keep the daughters with them in the cities. This is because they trained the daughters in the ways of a Mystic.

They are here and soon will appear again. Some of you feel drawn to them because you once were one in another lifetime. We will now bring forth their sacred names once again. Some of you will feel drawn to selected names. We ask that you respect the light of the Creator in them, for they respect the light of the Creator within you.

## Queens

Amara
BuKana *(Valkyrie)*
Freidja *(Valkyrie)*
Busknara
Darra
MuKara
NoRa

SeKora
Tora
ZenayaTuMora *(ZeMo)*

## Priestesses
Zeidya
Zedya
Zenya

## Valkyries
Net/Athena
Furna
Muana
Nowena
Sarena
Sorena
Tamona
Torwana
Ulvena
Unmana
Zana
Zurtana

## Pegasus Masters
Pelketa
Zetta
Zushkuta

## Archers

BeRaTe
Du'KaTe
FrethaNaTe
Geote
*They were guardians of the city gates*

## Guards/Warriors

Acydica
Aithia
Asynjor
Biska *(Princess: BuKana's daughter)*
CarTuMaKe
CarTuMeKesh
Fracu
Fuire
Gurthie
GeorgathaKa *(Princess)*
Hii
Hycynthia
KaTa
KasheNaMartu
Keliotye
Kee
Llami
Mursa
Ooku
PerKetha

Ruome
Ratine
RusheKa *(Princess: Zemo's daughter)*
Rachek
SashesKa *(Princess: Zemo's daughter)*
SorNoa
Tuthome
Tur
Toshema
Zanae
ZurKunyWa

# <u>Victory</u>

*Goddess Nike at the ruins of the ancient Greek city of Ephesus, Turkey*

The goddess Nike is associated with holding a rowan wreath and a reed. The reed is associated with the Scorpio segment upon the Zodi wheel. This signifies the serpent fire, which is your Soul. The reed is seen in ancient Celtic Druid teachings as the symbol of the

115

Soul. It is taught that Scylla *(sea serpent)*, Zelus *(fiery)*, Via/Bia *(force),* and Kratos *(power)* are siblings of Nike, in reality these are simply aspects. These all signify a personality held within your own serpent fire. The other siblings spoken of are Fontes *(fountains)* and Lacus *(Lakes)* which merely signify your Soul stream where you drink your own serpent fire.

As seen in the Zodi wheel, the rowan tree is associated with the Capricorn segment. This is connected to the crowning one receives when their ascension is engaged. The word *cap* is found in Capricorn for this reason. The color of wild corn is seen as purple, which signifies the Christos energy. Corn is also associated with the harvesting of the Soul.

The rowan tree is called *Sorbus* in Latin; it is from *sor* that you get the meaning red. This is where red associated with the holiday Christmas comes from. It is truly the name Nik this archetype essence holds. From Nik you find the name Nicolas, who is associated with the same holiday. The Christmas tree signifies the lightning up of your Kundalini or all Chakras needed before you can become crowned by the Christos.

It is not that a physical man was "crucified" on a rowan tree like spoken of in the more recent years, it simply signifies your own Christos light bound within the in-between. What we mean by this is that field of energy where the Seen and Unseen Worlds do not exist. This is outside of time yet also inside of time. It is within existence yet outside of existence. We speak in riddles for this is a codded transmission meant for you to decipher not with the mortal mind. The legends spoken of do not literally mean any of that which is used by the tongue to express. It is only from that which is unheard and from that which is unseen can you find the answers that you seek beautiful sparks of THE LIGHT.

The term victory is associated with this god archetype. Yet, what does that mean to you? Victory in the English tongue expresses an achievement of MASTERY. When you subtract the energy fields that the mortal resides in, you will discover that this does not mean an achievement of war. Victory means to become a victor of your own internal battle. It means to overcome that of the seen realms, to become a master and fly upon the golden sandals into the Gateway of the Sun.

Nike seen in the right hand of Zeus signifies this that we speak of. Even though many teachings have been physically destroyed, you all hold those textbooks within your own essence. Seek within, that which you have been seeking without.

*Pheidias's statue of Zeus at Olympia, 1815 Quatremere de Quincy*

In the next image you will notice the goddess Nike offering an egg to a snake. Remembering that the egg signifies your Christ Seed *(See **The Grain** Chapter)* and the serpent signifies your Soul, this is the engagement of the sacred crowning. The column that the snake is wrapped around signifies your reed *(spine/kundalini/Jacob's Ladder)*. Adorned atop the

118

column is goddess Athena. Knowing now that the reed is associated with Scorpio, take note that on the Zodi wheel you will also find an owl.

*Nike Warrior*

The owl is seen as a symbol associated with Athena. Owls are seen as wise because when you are Crowned by Nike, you have become a Master. The warrior seen to the right in the image is that victor. The word victory is connected to the word weik which is where you get wick/wik/witch. The rowan tree is known as the wik tree/the wigan tree/the witch tree. It is because of this fractured teaching that you see how far a stream has separated from the original ocean. The

119

original ocean of teachings once taught in the ancient temples.

When you look at the archetypes associated with the rowan tree, you will find that they all are paired with a thunder god. It is because thunder is always followed by the light. The egg is a representation of the Light Seed that comes with a flash of lightning. The lightning is alongside her siblings of force *(Via)* and power *(Kratos)* seen as thunder. Sometimes her other siblings seen as the rain *(Lacus and Fontes)* join in to play.

# Athena

*Birth of weaponed Athena, between 550-525 BC*

Athena is known to be birthed from Zeus's forehead after swallowing her mother Metis. The essence of Metis signifies a dream. Athena emitting from Zeus's forehead signifies a thought form. Just how all of creation started as a thought from THE MIND, so did all of that created in the Universe of Form. Athena represents the essence of all elixirs created from the mind of Zeus.

Understanding now the true meaning of victory, how it is not associated with a physical war, one can now understanding why Athena is associated here. The symbols of armor, a spear, and a helmet are all connected to victory. The essence of Athena will be ignited atop of the head by Nike when you become the victor.

The olive tree is associated with Athena due to the essence of olive oil. This is the very oil that drips into your spine when your oil lamp is lit. That sacred honey which is only accessed via your own Christos light. Your physical body is the lamp. Your 9th Chakra *(located at the base of the skull, thalamus area)* is the pouring hole of the lamp. Your Crown Chakra is the wick hole and the nozzle. Your thalamus is the fuel chamber.

121

Your thalamus is the great temple in receiving the abundance of your Soul from the great garden of creation. The very gold dust gifted to this garden of form was and is emitted from Zeus. This is seen in the symbolism of Athena and why we call it Athena's teachings. The many temples in Athena's honor are because of this.

Located in the temporal lobe, which is in the cerebral cortex of your physical brain, is the hippocampus. The word temple is seen in the word temporal. This is termed this because it sends signals into your thalamus, that pyramid of light.

*As light enters your Crown Chakra, it travels directly into the Corpus Callosum and is stored in your Thalamus. The Corpus Callosum is very important because the two hemispheres of the brain are energetically becoming one.*

*The way it works is light enters into the white matter (largest white matter formation in the brain) of the Corpus Callosum to be received by myelinated axons. These are the nerve fibers that can send signals to the body faster. They are covered with a lipid sheath, and this is what makes them myelinated. There are over 200 million of them in your Corpus Callosum. These nerve fibers are key players at making sure the two brain hemispheres communicate.*

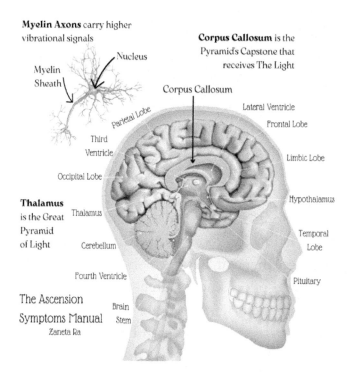

Myelin Axons carry higher vibrational signals

Nucleus

Myelin Sheath

Corpus Callosum is the Pyramid's Capstone that receives The Light

Corpus Callosum

Lateral Ventricle

Parietal Lobe

Frontal Lobe

Third Ventricle

Limbic Lobe

Occipital Lobe

Hypothalamus

Thalamus is the Great Pyramid of Light

Thalamus

Temporal Lobe

Cerebellum

Fourth Ventricle

Pituitary

The Ascension Symptoms Manual
Zaneta Ra

Brain Stem

*Think of the Corpus Callosum as a white capstone that receives plasma light. This light is sent into the Thalamus which acts as a pyramid. This is the secret of the Crown Chakra. When your Crown*

*Chakra opens it allows this capstone to activate and that causes a lot of head symptoms.*

*~ The Ascension Symptoms Manual*

---

The figure seen as Zeus-Ammon with horns is connected to the hippocampus because of this light pathway. The Egyptian aspect is seen sometimes with a ram's head because the spiral of the horns signifies the spiral of creation. It is a thought wave emitted out like a capillary wave. It is from this gigantic spiral that the Universe of Form came into fruition.

The entire Universe is the grand garden. The golden pollen that is gifted to the seeds of that garden is gifted by the Athena archetype along with many others. One of these other known archetypes is the Celtic Sulis. Sulis in the original tongue means *golden* or *sun*. This was a reference to the sun body once receives when their lamp is lit.

Sulis is also known as Sulis Minerva due to their solar deity connection alongside Athena. The Minerva aspect is also seen with the owl, olive tree, helmet, spear, and serpent symbols. Once again this is all connected to the Scorpio segment on the Zodi wheel.

The scorpion is seen with a stinger because when you have the Christos breathed into you, it feels like an instance sting. It is in that very moment that your flesh turns into light. You feel the burst of hot heat that gives you a pleasure no human sensation can measure.

*Scorpion men encountered by Gilgamesh, 1900, drawn by Faucher-Gudin* {{PD-US}}

The scorpion beings were seen in ancient teachings as the guardians to the Gateway of the Sun. In the image you will notice the egg along with the winged sun. This is associated with the serpent breath segment on the Zodi wheel. These god archetypes merely signify

125

the macro essence as the guardians of the sacred honey used to help the "seeds" grow.

*Zaneta Ra:* The Soul in Bondage image represents the transformation they speak of. The butterfly placed on the hand symbolizes that your transformation is navigated by your own hand. The Sun portal seen in the background can only be flown into by you.

*Soul in Bondage, Elihu Vedder, 1891-1892*

# God Aspects

*Zaneta Ra:* These are the aspects that wish to come forward for the purpose of this book. They wish to clarify what their essence originally was created to be. There are unlimited aspects as well as labels given to them from the mortals. When an aspect comes to you, look at the underlying spiritual meaning of their essence. Most make the mistake of feeding their ego by emerging themselves with that essence as their own identity. We are all essences and all personalities. The information in this section is fully channeled directly from the God Worlds.

## Agayu
An aspect of Earth's tectonic plates and all energy connected to them such as volcanic eruptions.

*Symbols:* Bulls, roosters, and the color red.

## Agassou

An aspect of the leopard species. Just like any aspect, he will appear sometimes as a leopard.

*Symbols:* Leopard and the golden hues like that of a leopard.

## Agathodeamon

An aspect of protection *(hence the name deamon)* and healing. The original meaning of the word Agatho means to unite or to coil, this is where the coiled serpent seen as his manifestation stems from.

*Symbol:* Serpent.

## Agni

An aspect of the Sun. Agni means fire however, originally this is the Ra fire, as in that which is used to transform the flesh into light.

*Symbols:* The Sun, lightning, and the colors of the Sun at dawn.

## Ana/Anu/Aine/An

An aspect of the feminine LIGHT that the Christ Seed is birthed from. Anu is known in Celtic as the mother of the Tuatha De Danaan. She is also seen as Saint

Anne, for they originate from the same teaching pond. This simply is the mother aspect along with Isis and any Mary titles. However, this title signifies the mother energy of the entire Universe of Form, meaning the mortal Earthly worlds. Ana is the one women garden that all "seeds" bloom from. The seeds seen here are the Christ Seeds provided to all of you. The title Mary originally was Meri, which means *pearl* and symbolizes your mother aspect which is your wholeness. All Souls were created as a fiery pearl. For more information on Meri please see **Rising Merits: The 42 Pearl Temples of Ancient Egypt.**

*Symbols:* The Sun, fire, rubies, and the color red.

## Ajysit

An aspect of birth and fertility.

*Symbols:* Cows, milk, and the color green.

## Alcyone

An aspect of the Throat Chakra energy center. Alcyone is seen as a kingfisher of your spirit because it signifies the messenger. Your voice is to be aligned and used for your spirit to speak through.

*Symbols:* Kingfisher bird and the color white.

## Aluluei

An aspect of cognizant, clear knowing. Aluluei houses all knowledge and wisdom because it simply is the energy channel connected directly to Source. The divine channel that all have access to if they so choose to.

*Symbols:* Stingray, two faces *(symbolizes the ability to see forward and backwards, all knowing),* and the colors black and white.

## Amaterasu

An aspect of illumination and reflection. Amaterasu is the light that shines into the windows of a home to illuminate all dust. Amaterasu will show you all of your aspects, those of the light and of the shadows. Amaterasu is the goddess of truth.

*Symbols:* Mirrors, Sun, bright light, and a sword.

## Ammit

An aspect that transmutes what no longer serves you. Ammit is seen as a dog that is waiting to eat, but this originally meant the essence that you give what no longer serves you to. He then will transmute it and recycle that energy out for the highest good of Creation.

*Symbols:* Crocodile, dog, or a dog with scales to weigh the energy.

## Amon

An aspect of Zeus/Odin, the giver of mortal life. Amon is seen as a ram because of the spiral horns. The very sound wave and thought wave emitted from Zeus was projected out like the horns of a ram. One denotes the creation of the Mortal Universe, and the other denotes the creation of the God Universe. The reason that the lamb is seen as a symbol of the Christos is because the lamb comes from a ram. The ram houses the seeds that is gifted to the mother garden. It is from this garden that little lambs expand and grow.

*Symbols:* Ram, shofar, bull, breath/wind, and the color blue.

## Anakhita

An aspect of the Higher Self. This is the pearl aspect that all incarnated Lower Self aspects emitted from. This can be a human incarnate or the planet Earth. Anakhita is seen to some as the planet Venus because Venus is the Higher Self of Earth. Anakhita will sometimes appear to those who are on their Ascension pathway.

*Symbols:* Venus, pearl, Sun, honey, roses, peacock, dove, and the color gold.

## Ananke

An aspect of destiny. Ananke merely represents the Divine Blueprint of what is to be. The very blueprint designed for the highest good of the overall Creator's Divine Will. Ananke will appear sometimes to those who desire to follow their destiny. She will let you know that you are on the right path. Even if you are not, the hands of time will move you. Those who incarnate with a very specific destiny that is designed to benefit all of Creation, Ananke will always be your guide.

*Symbols:* Time, clock, pathways, golden roads, and a spindle *(denotes weaving destiny).*

## Anansi

An aspect of a matrix. A matrix is a blueprint, or a play created from either the collective consciousness or the Higher Realms. This can be seen as a book of time.

*Symbols:* Storybook, spider, and a spider web *(the web denotes a matrix).*

## Antaura

An aspect of Astral voices. Antaura is the collective energy of all energies that reside within the Astral Plane. These are those whispers that enter mortal minds. The very whispers that manifest if they are given energy.

*Symbols:* Ghosts, wind, the sound of someone crying.

## Anubis

An aspect of the Underworld portal. Anubis is the one who allows passage from and to the Underworld, which is here. All Earthly Worlds are seen as the Underworld. When you are ready to ascend into your Higher Self, Anubis is the one who you will meet at the Halls of Judgment. This is where the weight of the heart and feather occurs. What this means is that in order to exit this realm, one cannot hold dense emotions in their heart. The heart must be light as a feather. The Ascension Teachings of healing the Emotional Body is key for anyone who desires to pass this portal gate. For more details on this god please reference the **Rising Merits** book.

*Symbols:* Guard dog, jackal, a knight in black armor, and the color black.

## Anuenue

An aspect of the portal into the Higher Realms. Anuenue is the aspect one uses to crossover from this world into the God Worlds or what some call Heaven. The mere representation of the "Rainbow Bridge".

*Symbols:* The Rainbow or all colors of light.

## Aphrodite

An aspect of the Christos energy. Existence is love, it is not an emotion, it simply IS. When love emits from the heart it creates gold dust which helps to pollinate existence. This is seen as the Christos energy.

*Symbols:* Beauty, roses *(the Christos blooms in the garden),* dove, the Sun, planet Venus, swan, and all animals that feed from a garden.

## Apollo

An aspect of the Christos energy. Apollo represents the food provided in the garden while his twin Artemis protects it.

*Symbol:* The Sun.

## Arachne

An aspect of Timekeepers. These are the energies that keep all timelines woven.

135

*Symbols:* Spiders, spider webs, thread, weaving, silk, spider lily, and the color purple.

*Arachne, Paolo Veronese, between 1575-1577*

## Ares

An aspect of the mortal battles. Ares is the essence that all experience while incarnated. The very battles a Soul faces and overcomes before becoming the victor. When the battle has been won, victory is gifted from the goddess essence of Nike.

*Symbols:* Warrior, sword, spear, helmet, shield, and the color red *(red is the crimson path all incarnated Souls truly walk)*.

## Arianrhod

An aspect of descending into the Mortal Worlds. Arianrhod is associated with the Moon or as known today a "silver wheel". There are two wheels in the realms of duality. The golden wheel is the Sun and represents Ascension. The silver wheel is the Moon and represents Descension. The original moon worshiping is for those who worship the mortal existence. The Moon is paired with night, sleeping, incarnation. Those who worship the Sun are worshiping day, awaken, Ascension out of the mortal form.

*Symbols:* The Moon and the color Silver.

## Asherah

An aspect of Ascending into the Sun. Asherah is the essence of day and light. The very essence one is awarded after transfiguring the mortal form. She can also be seen as the mother essence which is the Higher Self. It is from your Overself/Monad that the Higher Self emerges. Your Higher Self then births your Lower Self. It is because of this process that Asherah is seen to some as the lady of the water. The water represents the comic ocean waters that surround the child while in the womb. All mortals are in the womb of the mother. The mother is the garden, and you all are the seeds.

*Symbols:* The Sun, lion, dove, apples, and fruit trees.

## Atlas

An aspect of all material forms. Since Atlas is the combined essence of all the seen forms, he is the wisest of the Mortal Worlds.

*Symbol:* Always seen holding of the Earth. This symbolizes the fact that he IS the Earth. All material worlds are Earth.

## Baba Yaga

An aspect of incarnation. Baba Yaga is the essence used to incarnate. This is the transformation process used to go from life to death, which simply is a transformation. She is associated with the forest because to come into an Earthly incarnation is like going into the woods.

*Symbols:* Fire and Earth, because this is the process of exiting the light form and entering an Earthly form. Poppies, because they cause you to "sleep". Existing in the Mortal Worlds is simply existence within a dream. All animals, because they are associated with the Earth.

## Bastet

An aspect of the essence of life itself. Bastet is associated with felines because the man body was molded by the Seraphim. The Seraphim's first man body houses feline-like features upon the face. It is because of this first creation for this Universal Body that the feline is seen as life. Some humans today can be seen with feline-like features. When beings from other star systems came during Egypt, they were seen with black lined eyes. The Egyptians would line their eyes in black charcoal to resemble those gods who came from the stars to teach them.

*Symbols:* All felines, ankh, the color green, the Sun and the Moon *(they symbolize life, day and night).*

## Belenus

An aspect of the Christos energy. Belenus is seen as the bright white shining one which merely is the Christos essence.

*Symbols:* The Sun, fire, and a white horse.

## Bia

An aspect of the essence of force. Bia is seen as the sibling of Nike because this essence is needed in order to obtain victory.

*Symbols:* Anything that denotes force, power, and strength.

# Brigid

An aspect of the communication system from the Light Body to the brain. Brigid is seen with a serpent coiled around the crown as a symbol of this communication essence. The serpent fire is the pathway of the light from your Soul into the mortal form. Therefore, many ancient temples had the serpent symbols to denote this meaning. Brigid is connected to both the Gemini segment on the Zodi wheel and Virgo. Zeus previously mentioned that he is also Dagda, which is the father aspect of Brigid. When the word father is used today it is seen as a parent. In the ancient teachings the word used was something equivalent to a creator, with a lower case "c". That term then became known as "god", then the word "father".

*Symbols:* Fire, a pillar of fire, white cow, a red cow, white horse, a white bull, a red bull, and a spindle. The white animal signifies your higher essence where the red animal represents the mortal form.

# Celaeno

An aspect of the Root Chakra. Celaeno is one of the seven sisters known together as the Pleiades. This name is associated with animals due to their connection with the Mortal Kingdom. Keep in mind that man is also part animal in nature. It is because of this connection that her son Lycus means "wolf", which simply is one of the energies emitted from the Root Chakra. When you start your ascension process, the Root Chakra is the first to dissolve. This is because you are eliminating that animal essence to return into the light essence.

*Symbols:* Animals and the color red.

## Cliodna

An aspect of the Higher Crystal Heart. Cliodna is said to be the goddess of love and healing. It is said that she oversees the land of paradise. This is because your Higher Crystal Heart is this paradise. Once this is anchored within you, your entire realty becomes a paradise. All that you feel and see is beauty. Her connection to the number three symbolizes the tri-fold flame that all Souls are created with. The crystal pyramid that connects the lower essences of the Soul with Divine Creator.

*Symbols:* Songbirds, hearts, and the number 3.

## Cupid

An aspect of the internal fire, the Ra. Cupid is the harmonized light of both chaos and love within the

141

mortal. The concept of Cupid shooting into the heart signifies the activation of the Light Seed. All Immortal Souls were given a Light Seed which is located within their Blue Pearl *(Christ Seed)*. When this is fully activated it sends one into an instant bliss state. The legends saying that Cupid is from both Mars *(chaos)* and Venus *(love)* denotes the balance needed for Ascension. This is where the birth of Cupid's child Voluptas comes from. Voluptas is the energy emitted from your Christ Seed, it is pure bliss.

*Symbols:* Heart, bow and arrow, and the color red.

## Cybele

*Plate depicting Cybele alongside Nike, a votive sacrifice and the sun god, 3rd century BC*

An aspect of Divine Abundance. Cybele is seen with a cornucopia filled with food, signifying abundance. The food simply represents substance fed to your Soul. This substance comes from the Divine Mother. It merely is the gold dust from the Mighty Beehive that is fed to all of Creation. Cybele is seen with Nike to bring forth the abundance fed into the mortal from at the time Nike performs the Crowning of enlightenment.

*Symbols:* Bees, roses, lions, honey, and the colors yellow and gold.

## Dagda

An aspect of a light god such as Zeus or Odin. There is a light and a shadow god that resides within each God World. It is originally from Dagda that the term "Dad" stems.

*Symbols:* A harp, cauldron, and a club.

## Dai Nichi

An aspect of the Sun. Dai Nichi merely represents the great illuminator that sustains all life in this Solar System.

*Symbols:* Light, the Sun, brightness, and sometimes a golden lotus.

## Damona

An aspect of the Mother Universe, the garden. Damona is the essence of this Universe, which is known as the garden, it is because of this she is associated with wheat. Ancient teachings taught that wheat grew from the crown of the human to touch the heavens. It grows as a golden light from the Christ Seed *(located in the thymus/8th Chakra).* She is also seen as a cow, just like Hathor, which again signifies the great Mother. Milk is fed to the child from the Mother and this is why cows were used to signify a mother essence. The Mother in this sense refers to the Universal Body we all exist within. It is the Universe that feeds us so our mortal forms can live.

*Symbols:* Cow, milk, and wheat.

## Electra

An aspect of the Sacral Chakra. Electra is one of the seven sisters known as the Pleiades. Electra was used to express the amber color hue that is emitted from this energy center *(Chakra).*

*Symbol:* Any color within the amber spectrum, especially orange.

144

# Enki

An aspect of overseer of Earth. The title ENKI is not pertaining to a name. EN in the original tongue means *"Head of"* and KI means *"Earth"* as in *Head of the Earthly Worlds*. This is not an individual as seen upon Earth but as a collective energy. The organic nature of this title has been misconstrued and fractalized over time.

*Symbols:* None. This essence does not appear but to select few and has no form or connection to manifestations found upon the Earthly Worlds. What this essence wishes to express is that the mortal is unable to fully comprehend "it".

# Fauna

An aspect of sacred wisdom.

*Symbols:* Cornucopia and a snake.

# Fortuna

An aspect of automatic abundance. Fortuna is another goddess seen holding a cornucopia. She is the essence that represents the Law of Action. What this means is the abundant energy you vibrate out will boomerang back to you via the Universal Laws. It was not taught as a law of attraction but a Law of Action. It is through your own actions that this energy is dispersed. An action can be seen as a thought, spoken word, a physical action as well as an unspoken word or a nonaction. It is all energy; however, some is done consciously and some unconsciously. Just because someone "thinks" they are performing an act of service does not mean the Universe will receive it that way. If the vibrations presented at the time of that act are not aligned with the action being performed, then it is not valid. Performing an act of service should simply flow through us all and not be performed with the intent of it being reciprocated. Being a true *service to others* archetype simply **IS**. One does not think before they perform a kind act because they are one with that energy already. It is because of this unification that fortune is gifted via the essence of Fortuna or as some call her "Lady Luck".

*Fortuna balancing the orb of sovereignty, 1520-1530, Artist is unknown,* {{PD-US}}

*Symbols:* Wheel of Fortune, cornucopia, an orb *(not a globe)*, and a wreath.

## Freyja

An aspect of a Valkyrie Angel. Freyja is a title of an Angel that escorts Souls out of the Earthly Worlds. Sometimes a Soul is ready to ascend, however, it is unable to due to the damage caused to their Light Body. To access the God Worlds portal, one must be of a certain vibration. When Souls enter a portal, they will transport to a realm that is a match to their vibrational field. What this means is that someone of a higher vibration can escort someone of a lower vibration because the higher vibration is what the portal system matches to, not the lower vibrations. Souls who had a lot of emotional traumas typically need this kind of escort. They are taken to a realm for healing and repair to their Light Body. If the Light Body is not taken care of *(in this realm and there)*, it can actually cause the entire Soul to dissolve. Therefore, allowing emotions to simply flow is the key to a healthy Light Body.

*Symbols:* Warrior Angel, gold helmet, primroses, large felines, honey, and a falcon.

## Gabija

An aspect of ashes. Gabija is associated with ashes in a sense of transformation. The light that enters the mortal form will transform the flesh into light, leaving behind ashes *(skin cells as they shed away)*. This process can also be linked to the cracking of the chrysalis when the butterfly breaks free. The caterpillar crawls into the chrysalis and becomes a butterfly. When it uses its own strength to break free, the chrysalis falls to the Earth like ashes when you rise as a phoenix during ascension.

*Symbols:* Ashes, fire, hearth, snake *(due to the sheading of its skin),* and the color red.

## Ganesha

An aspect of anew. Ganesha is associated with new beginnings and depicted today with an elephant's head. The elephant is known for its horn sounding trunk. The sound blown is likened to the sound blown in a shofar *(rams' horn)*. Creation itself was created by sound. The connection here is that when you are aligned to your light, you can paint any reality you desire. The blank canvas sits before you and Ganesha will blow his horn to allow your desires to manifest upon it. This sound is known also as the trumpet sounding.

*Symbols:* Hearing a horn in your sleep, axe, lotus, elephant, and the colors of pink *(including those that create this color such as red/white).*

## Green Man

*How I see him, from the book **Love Letters from Lemuria***

An aspect of trees. The Green Man is the collective consciousness of all the tress. He usually appears to Gridworkers and any Light Worker that works with the Nature Kingdom. He also allows passage into the Inner Worlds *(Avalon, Inner Earth etc.)* via trees.

*Symbols:* Vines, Ivy, anything thing that grows from the Earth that is green, and oak trees.

## Hathor

An aspect of the Mother of the Material Realms. The name Hathor is transcribed from ancient Egyptian *ḥwt-ḥr*. Hwt in the original tongue means *temple* or *sound* and is where the word hut comes from. Hr means *surface* or *in sight*. An ancient hut is round on the bottom with a slightly pointed top. This represents the spiraling sound waves emitting from the mouth of the Divine Mother. These spiraling waves of plasma heat spun and spun until they cooled creating the material worlds. The sistrum is associated with Hathor to denote how sound created the Material Worlds. For more details on this goddess please reference the **Rising Merits** book.

*Symbols:* Cow, lilies, sistrum, Moon, malachite stone, date palm, sycamore tree, and the color gold.

## Hermes

An aspect of a sacred messenger. Hermes is not just one being but several. Hermes signifies an Oracle who travels from the physical planes to the hidden planes as a messenger. The golden winged sandals are used to travel from Earth into the Sun City Pearlia *(See* **Angelic Pearls 144** *book for more on Pearlia)*. This city is known to some as the realm of Asgard, the city surrounded by fiery walls.

*Symbols:* Winged sandals, caduceus, honey, and a palm tree.

## Horus

An aspect of a time portal. Horus simply is the essence of a time portal used to exit the current time matrix. This is typically used at the time of transcending via a physical or non-physical ascension process. The word hour stems from Horus. An hourglass is shaped like a time portal as well. For more details on this god please reference the **Rising Merits** book.

*Symbols:* Time, hourglass, eye *(symbol for a time portal),* falcon, and a hawk.

## Huaina

An aspect of Earth wisdom. Huaina is the goddess archetype of the wisdom that is encoded within all of Earth. She comes to some in the form of goddess Daina. Daina is a form she used to appear to humans as a teacher in the ancient temples. This information has been destroyed over 8,000 linear years ago and she asked for her to be brought forth again. Daina merely is the library of Earth. Huaina represents the real organic records of man and Earth.

*Symbols:* Quill, library, scrolls, white scepters that hold information, and sometimes as a green crystal skull.

# Inanna

An aspect of your Higher Self. Inanna represents your Higher Self. Venus as stated previously, is the Higher Self of Earth and denoted by the 8th Chakra. When the 8th Chakra ignites, the Christ Seed is seeded from your Higher Self into your higher heart. Your physical four-chambered heart starts to form as an eight-petal crystalline heart. The Christ Seed *(also known as the blue pearl)* is in the center of the higher heart which creates the rosette shape. The planet Venus and the 8-pointed star associated with Inanna is because of this. The ancient temples of Inanna-Ishtar was for humans to learn how to expand their heart for this process. The depictions of Inanna taming lions refer to the roar of the mortal mind. It is when the mind is quiet that one can hear the whispers of their Soul.

*Symbols:* Venus, 8-pointed star, rosette, dove, crown of stars, and the color blue *(for the blue pearl/Christ Seed)*.

# Isis

An aspect of your Higher Self. When the initiate passes through the Horus time portal, they meet with Isis and Osiris. Osiris is the Christos essence and Isis is the Higher Self essence. When your merge with your Christos light you then marry your Higher Self. This is the final stage of Ascension and the grand INTERAL Solar Flash that is drawn out in the Book of the Dead.

Isis as the winged sun symbolizes this process. For more details on this please reference the **Rising Merits** book.

*Symbols:* Winged sun, honey, Virgo *(reference the Zodi wheel)*, holding a child *(your incarnated self)*, and the color gold.

## Janus

An aspect of the Sun Gateway. The god Janus is what the month January was named after. He is the god of time, new beginnings, endings, doorways, transitions, as well as duality. There are many major gateways for the Earth, however, he oversees the main gate called The Sun Door. This is the gateway that leads Souls to the Solar Gates. The god Janus is seen sometimes with two heads because this doorway is made of two doors. Just like all doorways into the God Realms they will have two doors, where the ones to the mortal homes have one door.

The Souls that do not house the Key Codes upon their Light Body to go directly to the Sun City Pearlia will have to travel via this gateway to enter the Sun. Why is this process of importance? It is important because this is how a Soul can leave this local Solar System. The gates there are like that of Grand Central Station. There are many routes one can take to exit the "city".

*Symbol:* Doors.

## Juno

An aspect of time. Juno is the feminine aspect of an era in time. Juno is the Roman aspect of the Greek Hera. Hera is partnered with Zeus, where Juno is paired with Jupiter. When the Jupiter/Zeus essence went to plant the "seeds" into the "garden", eras of time were needed to separate them. This is seen as rows in a garden. Each row is an era of time.

*Symbols:* Peacocks, crows, iris, wolves, snakes, and lions.

## Jupiter

An aspect of Zeus.

*Symbols:* Eagle, oak tree, and lightning.

## Kahoupokane

An aspect of the snow.

*Symbol:* Snowflakes.

## Kali Ma

An aspect of the Ra fire. Kali Ma is the same as the Ra, which can be used to create or destroy. This aspect was used long ago to teach humans how to become a master at this energy. The energy of today's emotions can be harnessed and refocused to create the Ra energy. This process was once taught in the ancient temples and mystery schools.

*Symbols:* Mirrors, cauldron, skulls, crows, and the colors black and red.

## Ladon

An aspect of the guardian energy that guards the Tree of Life for this Universal Body. Ladon is spoken of as a dragon serpent that guards the golden apples of the gods. The golden apples *(and oranges)* are the Christos light, the sacred Divine Wisdom. This wisdom is gifted to those of the Mortal Worlds when they ascend into the God Worlds. Ladon is known by many labels and seen in different stories as the serpent that guards the "wisdom tree" of the "garden".

*Symbols:* A snake wrapped around a giant tree. Sometimes a snake wrapped around a golden apple.

## Lady of the Lake

An aspect of a Divine Messenger, usually galactic. The Lady of the Lake is usually seen wearing a light blue dress and ascending from water. She has long blonde hair and blue eyes. When she emits from the water, she is typically holding a sacred trinket. This trinket is something encoded with Light Codes for you to do Divine Work. She is most known as delivering a sword which simply is the tongue, meaning Divine Will of God Source. She can come to you with a scepter in in her hand that is yours in another planet/timeline. When she appears to me, she is a sacred deity from the Pleiades system, equivalent to a goddess here. There is not one Lady. Those who have a Divine Mission may have this sacred messenger appear as any deity. The deity that appears will be one known to your Soul.

*Symbols:* Sword, scepter, the color blue, a blue lake under the moon light with small blue orbs.

## Lakshmi

An aspect of the Crowning. Lakshmi represents the goddess energy that ignites your Crown energy center so your Higher Self can descend. The lotus symbol she uses represents the Crown Chakra opening, as well as the Higher Heart. The petals of the lotus expanding is the representation of this initiation.

*Symbols:* Lotus, fruit, pink flowers, gold flowers, white flowers, cow, elephant, and sometimes basil.

## Leigong

An aspect of the God Portal. Lei Shen is the same as the famous god Tor/Thor. This represents the portal that Souls use to exit the Mortal Worlds and enter the God Worlds. He also protects the pure ones.

*Symbols:* The hammer and a drum. The drum *(shaped like an hourglass)* is the symbol of the doorway. Picture two pyramids with the top points touching. Where they touch is the doorway.

## Leprechaun

An aspect of protectors of the Christ consciousness. The rainbow represents the portal used during Ascension. The gold at the end is the golden body, the Christ body or known as the Christ consciousness. This is the gown worn during the time Mastery is received. Mastery gained from conquering the Worlds of Form. Leprechauns are male fairies basically that protect this "gold". They also can be messengers that help lead you to it. Green is the color of "The Garden" and represents birthing because at this level, you are being reborn.

*Symbols:* Four-leaf clover, pot of gold, the colors green and gold.

## Lugh

An aspect of your Christos essence. Lugh is the Celtic god known as the "Bright One" and seen as a Sun. The Sun represents the Christos essence of yourself just as the god Osiris does.

*Symbols:* The Sun, the colors of the Sun at sunrise, raven, and a white horse *(usually in your dreams, signifies that your Christos essence is calling to you).*

## Maia

An aspect of the Crown Chakra. From Maia emitted Hermes, who simply is wisdom itself. Maia represents the Crown Chakra essence that emits wisdom into your incarnate essence.

*Symbols:* Staff, gold scroll, gold star, laurel wreath, and a gold crown.

## Mazu

An aspect of The Garden. Mazu is a special goddess because she was an actual incarnation of the essence of this Universal Body in a mortal form. The meaning of the sea is the Underworld, as in the Worlds of Form. The mother essence in whole, meaning that of the Material Universe *(The Garden),* sent a portion of its light into a human form. Many during her incarnation saw this light and felt it. This is why so many worship and honor her to this day. She transformed the physical form and returned all its elements back to the Universe. When she came into form it helped to anchor very important Light Codes for the Earth's organic blueprint.

*Symbols:* Lighthouse, the sea at sunrise, waves, and anything related to the Ocean.

## Mabon ap Modron

An aspect of your Christos essence. Mabon is known as the "divine child" because this is the Christos essence birthed from the virgin mother, your Higher Self. Mabon is the Celtic version of the essence known as Apollo or Maponus. This god is associated with the autumn equinox because this is when the harvest takes place. The harvest is seen spiritually as the Ascension.

*Symbols:* Water spring, yellow flowers, the Sun, and the color gold.

## Medusa

An aspect of the portal mirror of reflection and wisdom. Medusa is one of three Gorgons. She is seen with many snakes upon her head because they represent wisdom. Each direction they point towards is symbolic to all of existence. When you look upon her, she will reflect to you what your truth is. The legends about people turning into stone is a spiritual metaphor and not a literal account of the events that took place. Not everyone can handle the truth of what they carry within themselves. Those who can and seek her for wisdom will receive it. It is only when one sits in silence with their own shadows and defeats their own demons, will they gain true understanding. This is when one gains wisdom of Creation and self. No one outside of self can ever do this for you. This is the sacred key to Mastery and self-discovery. Medusa helps to show you that you have the power in your hand, not in another's. Overcome the misconception that dark is bad with the understanding that it simply is you. Everything is a reflection to show us the Universal Truth of who we are. It is when we label energy that it causes a divide. Everything and everyone in existence is of THE LIGHT. Everything is both chaos and love. Simply FEEL with your heart and not with the physical eyes and mind, and you will unlock the doorways to all of existence.

*Symbols:* Serpents, lions, mirrors, mirrors with fire, and the fire element itself.

## Merope

An aspect of the Heart Chakra. She is seen as a bright light because your heart light is the lighthouse to help guide you during a storm. The storm here means the depths of the density. This is the stem of the legends speaking of Merope guiding lost sailors home. Are not all humans sailors upon the Sea of life? The birthing of Glaukos from her is an ancient term for a bluish-green color. This is the light associated with the Heart Chakra.

*Symbols:* Bright white light, lighthouse, and a heart shape.

## Meriruka

An aspect of Zeus. Meriruka was a small light spark of the god Zeus that incarnated in Egypt. Meriruka was a Pearl Priest that taught others how to feed the Christos body.

*Symbols:* Staff and the hyena.

## Modron

An aspect of your Higher Self. Modron is seen as the virgin mother of the god essence Mabon. Mabon, as mentioned prior, is the essence of your Christos. Whenever legends speak of something being born, it means that it descended or factualized from it. Mabon being born of Modron symbolizes how the Christos light descended from the virgin essence, the white light body, which is your Higher Self, to incarnate in a physical body.

*Symbols:* Cauldron *(the mother symbol because it symbolizes something being "created"),* white light, and the constellation Virgo.

## Morgan le Fay

*Morgan le Fay, 1863-1864, Frederick Sandys*

An aspect of The Garden. Mor originally was Muir which means *Sea* and Gan means *mouth.* Understanding now that the Sea represents the Underworld; the mouth denotes the birthing. The Sea flowing from the mouth represents sound waves of the Divine Will spoken. As these waves spiral out, they cool and become a material form. This material form is The Garden which is the Universal Body of the Earthly Worlds. Morgan le Fay is the essence, the Divine Aspect of this in its totality. In the prior image you will see at the trim of her apron a backwards Z between two circles. This is seen on many ancient ruins because it denotes the God Portal. The Tor Portal that is used to travel from the Worlds of the Unseen and the Worlds of the Seen. The dress in this image is green to depict The Garden, life, as well as resurrection. Just like the goddess Mazu, Morgon le Fay also incarnated as the essence of The Garden. To help fix some of the inorganic disturbances in the DNA of man many divine essences incarnate *(See **Angelic Pearls 144** book for more information)*. The main reason this helps DNA is through paragenetics. When this Light Seed enters a human form, their light filters through that DNA lineage both forwards and backwards in time. This in-turn helps to heal Timelines.

---

*Timelines work in spirals with points of crossing. Where these points cross are portals that create opportunities to jump either up or down in frequency of that reality. Therefore, when your light ripples out to the "past", it can activate your ancestor, who is at that crossing point, to jump up in frequency. This, in turn, will cause you to jump up several octaves. By that ancestor expanding in their light, it has a domino effect to those around them in that specific environment.*

*~Zaneta Ra*

*Cracking the Chrysalis: Shattering the Steps of Ascension*

---

*Symbols:* Cauldron, serpent, crow, waves, mermaid, really anything she wishes and especially that of the Fae World.

## Neith

An aspect of The Void. There are many Neiths but we speak of the original one and the only one, all others were titles used in ancient Egypt. Neith represents **No-Thing** as in the void that the original Light birthed from. Before The Creator came into as Source, there was nothing. Nothingness is the essence of infinity.

Neith can be seen as masculine because all of Creation was "seeded" from Neith. Neith can be seen as feminine because all of Creation was "birthed" from Neith. Neith is both masculine and feminine. Neith is you, is me, is we, is ALL and NOTHING.

*Symbol:* Darkness/nothing.

## Okuninushi

An aspect of land.

*Symbols:* Land, dirt, and rabbits.

## Pachacamac

An aspect of time and space.

*Symbols:* Clocks, time portals, hourglasses, and images of the Universe.

## Pasiphae

An aspect of the Higher Mind. Pasiphae merely represents the light that illuminates your mind. The stories of her producing the Minotaur are symbolic to the Lower Mind. The Lower Mind is the mortal mind and is why the Minotaur is seen with a man's body and a bull's head. The stories speak of her mating with a bull. The bull is seen as Taurus upon the Zodi wheel, which is the mortal mind. This again is an ancient teaching that wondered far from its original meaning.

*Symbols:* Bulls, minds, goose, and garland.

# Persephone

*Statue of syncretic Persephone-Isis with a sistrum. Roman period (180-190 CE). Heraklion Archaeological Museum, Crete, no changes made (**CC BY-SA 3.0**)*

An aspect of the feminine essence of the Underworld. Persephone is seen in this image with a parabola curve and a disc in the center *(crown)*. This symbolizes the portal into the Underworld, the Mortal Worlds. In her hand is a sistrum *(ancient tuning fork)* that symbolizes attunement and sound. She is affiliated with Isis to symbolize the Higher Self. Her connection to Hades simply is the shadow aspect of the Higher Self. It is only when we love both the light and shadow aspects of ourselves can we "attune" our frequency back to its organic nature. It is this organic nature that helps to open your internal solar gateway. The gateway needed so your Higher Self can descend while you ascend. When the two meet, a grand internal solar flash emits. This is when the marriage with your Christos essence occurs.

Her mother is Demeter which symbolizes the grain; therefore, Persephone is connected to the harvesting. It is because of this connection that she can be seen holding a wheat stalk in her hand. She is sometimes seen holding a pomegranate because this is the symbol of the unification of the Christos and the Higher Self. It is the symbol of Ascension. It signifies the death of the mortal essence and its rebirth into the light.

*Symbols:* Any kind of grain bundled, spring flowers, Springtime, a pomegranate, and dark purple.

## Pleiades

An aspect of the seven lower energy centers, Chakras. Depicted in the image before **The Grain** chapter are:

Maia-*Crown Chakra*
Sterope-*Third Eye Chakra*
Alcyone-*Throat Chakra*
Merope-*Heart Chakra*
Taygete-*Solar Chakra*
Electra-*Sacral Chakra*
Celaeno-*Root Chakra*

Chakras are like air vents in your home. As energy is filtered into your Light Body, it travels into your Physical Body by way of energy centers labelled Chakras. The essence of the Chakras for all of the Mortal Worlds is denoted by the Pleiades. When it comes to the Star System *(Ashkara in the native tongue)*, this was used long ago to distinguish where an energy source stream came upon Earth. An energy source stream is always sent into the lower Chakras to help increase its light quotient. This also was used at that time to denote many teachers who came from that system to help raise the planetary consciousness. This was during a time node of great importance that directly connects to the current one.

*Symbols:* See each name for their own symbols for they do not have a collective one.

## Sterope

An aspect of the Third Eye. Sterope means lightning because this energy center illuminates your reality as well as your Lower Mind. One of her children is said to be Hippodamia, the master of horses. The master of horses signifies the racing of the mortal mind. Hippodamia was birthed to help tame that racing horse of the mortal mind. When the Third Eye is illuminated it helps to dissolve the loud voices of the Ego. Sterope is the essence of this stairstep upon the pathway of enlightenment.

# The Golden Chalice
The Ascension Symptoms Manual
Zaneta Ra

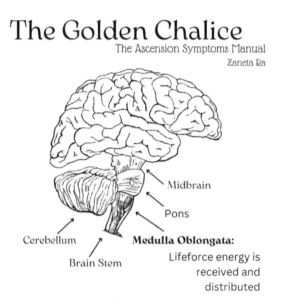

Cerebellum

Brain Stem

Midbrain

Pons

**Medulla Oblongata:**
Lifeforce energy is received and distributed

*Symbols:* An eye, white peacock *(she says the feathers extended signify the illumination of the light within the mind),* and a golden chalice *(for deeper understanding on* *the golden chalice see **The Ascension Symptoms Manual** book).*

*Zaneta Ra:* When Sterope said golden chalice, I looked confused. She then reminded me of the image I created of the golden chalice. What she means here is that when the Third Eye is illuminated, it allows the medulla oblongata to fill up. The light then pours down the brain stem and into your entire cellular structure. This is how people get "downloads" of information, especially those who are Clairvoyant *(clear seeing).* What happens is the light hits the cells with such intensity that you automatically have instant knowing *(Claircognizant).* In short terms, people call it instant DNA upgrades. Most assume it is always from Solar Flares, when the true sun is the internal one all have access to.

## Taygete

An aspect of the Solar Chakra. This is where the natural instincts are seeded. This energy is connected to animals and Artemis due to the stomach being your compass during the "hunt". The natural animal instincts that all humans have and call their gut.

*Symbols:* A hunter and an orange.

## Thoth/Thoout

An aspect of a thought-form *(Thoth-form)*. Thoth is mostly seen with an Ibis head, stylus, and a palette. The Ibis on the Zodi wheel symbolizes the Mental Body. The stylus and palette are the symbolization of your Mental Body and Emotional Body *(see the **Seeds of Mnemosyne** section)*. Sometimes he is seen as a baboon because this represents communication, as in mind chatter. Thoth is the Mental Body of the collective, which simply is the Astral Body. His aspect is connected to maintaining reality and wisdom, is this not what your Mental Body does for you?

*Symbols:* Ibis, stylus, palette, baboon, reed pens, scroll, and the color red.

## Voluptas

An aspect of enlightenment. Voluptas is the state of pure bliss which is emitted when the Christ Seed is activated. Light from the Light Seed located within it burst out pure fire throughout the physical vessel. This sends one into an instant orgasmic state. However, mastery is not achieved at that stage, this is only step one of many. Voluptas was birthed from Cupid and Psyche. Cupid signifies the internal fire where Psyche signifies the breath of life itself.

*Cupid and Psyche, 1798 by Francois Gerard* {{PD-US}}

*Symbols:* Pear and a pear tree *(hence the hidden symbolism in the saying of "a partridge and a pear tree", coded meaning from ancient past).*

172

# Excerpt from Angelic Pearls 144

## Goddess Themis

Themis means *divine law*, which she oversees as well as the balancing of the scales of justice. Her symbol is a sword just like many of the Archangels and those of the Melchizedek order are portrayed with. This is of the tongue, meaning the sword of truth. She works with oracles because a true oracle is one that is pure and has their pillar of light fully anchored from their Monad to their physical expression. An oracle is one that can communicate directly with the gods in the higher planes of Earth and the cosmos hence why the goddess of divine law works with them.

During the beginning of the Mu template, it was goddess Themis who led the Pearl temple teachings by training the High Priestesses. She is one of the gods those of the 5D Earth plane sought for rulings upon the lands. During the end of the Hyperborean template and the starting of Mu, a council of oracles was formed who would directly communicate with the gods of the

173

higher planes. These are the gods who oversaw not only Earth but all Earths, meaning material realms. Every planet in this solar system has material realms corresponding to an age upon the wheel of time. Musical spheres playing the notes selected to be by the Divine blueprint of Creation.

This was a time when others from the galaxy were coming to visit. They were coming from other 5D worlds to learn from these temples. It was during the end of the Mu template that Themis instructed the temple known today in Delphi to be formed. We must address that it is from the Titans that the Olympians were birthed. Just like from your very own Monad many Higher self aspects come, then from them many Lower self aspects. This merely is the meaning of the wars, for it was not truly a war but chaos. It is from chaos you as in the incarnate is form, it is from friction a cell can split from another. From Winter the delights of Spring can bloom. This is the true meaning of the scales of justice. The balancing of death and rebirth.

If there is an imbalance in creation, we of the Melchizedek order observe the grids to see where death is most beneficial and where rebirth is needed. Just how the Solarians measured the grid to see what vibrational Soul was needed to be of the highest good of the Divine plan for Earth's journey. The preselected voyage her Soul spark needed in order to expand. The very number of leaves needed to fall in one place to provide nutrients for the soil. Those leaves are you. Themis a Melchizedek, overseeing what energy needs to be extracted during the harvest of the universe. She is here now for she has never left, call upon her to guide you with discernment along your divine journey in this plane. Allow her to show you the Joan of Arc inside you all.

# Excerpt from Rising Merits

## Goddess Ari

Ari is known today as the goddess Ariadne. The story of Ariadne helping Theseus in the labyrinths to escape the Minotaur merely represents how she helps one to conquer the mind. The labyrinth represents the layers of the mind where the bull represents the voices chasing after you. In the story she gives Theseus a sword and a ball of red thread. The sword is your divine will, the sword of truth from your pearl-essence. The red thread is that pillar from your higher mind to be rooted into your mortal self. Red representing that firepower Ra energy you were created upon. Ariadne originally was *Arianna* meaning *lion of light*. Her Pearl Teachings in the temple were:

1-How to locate the labyrinth in the mortal mind.

2-How to conquer this maze and quiet the noise by escaping the bull.

3-How to open the gateway to allow the red pillar from your higher mind to become rooted.

4-How to lower the sword of truth into your heart and use it to cut the cords of what no longer serves you.

5-How to transmute the bull into the lion of light, your divine higher mind.

Legends say her consort was Dionysus. While Dionysus is the same as Osiris meaning your Christos light, it was not literally her male consort. In the original teachings the term was *Sahyun-su*. Sahyun later was transcribed into *Zion* and su into *sus*. All together this meant *hand of light*. The hand of light opens to gift you the divine wisdom of your higher mind. As the representation of palm trees igniting sparks of light, so does the fingers of your Higher self. Igniting into you sparks. Which are divine thoughts projecting in and out of you. From these very sparks you create. You paint onto your canvas the reality that serves your highest good.

# Excerpt from Cracking the Chrysalis

## Mystic Rose

When it comes to the phrase *"mystic rose"* we must look at the origin of this. The English word mystic stems from the Greek word *mústēs* which means *to initiate* or *one who has been initiated*. The single form of this word is *muéō* which means *I initiate*. The 144 tell me that the word rose originally was like the Arabic word *warda* which means *guardian* or *protector*. They informed me that it wasn't until later did this word also mean *flower* or *rose*. Therefore, the sacred legends of Mystic Rosehoods merely were for those who will become a guardian of sacred things.

A symbol affiliated with this is the famous rosette shape which later changed to a rose. The original rosette was a disk shape with 8 petals or leaves. Over time the number of petals changed. In ancient finds you will see 8 petals like in the Temple of Ramesses III

178

or ancient Sumerian finds. In Sumerian the 8 star is associated with the Goddess Ishtar and Venus. This is because Venus is the Higher Self of Earth.

It is when you ignite the 8th Chakra *(Higher Heart/Christ Seed)* that the rosette shield opens. This shield can be seen today in some church glass windows. It is by no accident the term Mystic Rose is seen as your Christ Seed. It is the Christ Seed that holds your organic Angelic Blueprint, the guardian. When this becomes ignited in your thymus area it emits out light codes via 8 crystalline chambers. These correspond to your T cells *(white blood cells in the thymus)*. It is your white blood cells that house your DNA not your red blood cells. T cells start in your bone marrow then are sent to your thymus to be fully formed.

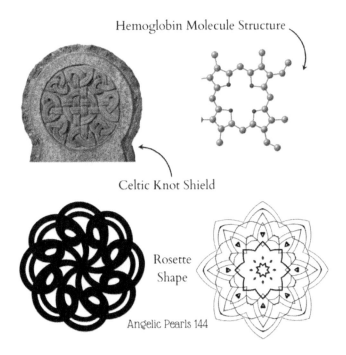

Hemoglobin Molecule Structure

Celtic Knot Shield

Rosette
Shape

Angelic Pearls 144

Your Higher Heart has eight chambers where your physical heart has four. Your $8^{th}$ Chakra is a key chain link to your pearl-essence. It has been proven that your T cells have an intelligence and communicate to your form. It is the T cells that determine when the physical vessel will completely shut down, meaning a physical termination. The T cells are receiving direct communication from your Monad *(Oversoul/Pearl Self)*.

# Other books by Zaneta Ra

**Advance Level Learning**

### Angelic Pearls 144
Pearl codes
from the
Seraphim
and the
Melchizedek
order
ISBN:
9798428688535

### Rising Merits
The 42 Pearl Temples
of Ancient Egypt
ISBN:
979-8804058464

**Intermediate Level Learning**

### Cracking the Chrysalis
Shattering
the Steps of
Ascension
ISBN:
9798840365298

### The Pearl Light Codes
44 Light Activations
from the Seraphim
ISBN: 9798438477693

# Introductory Level

**The Ascension
Symptoms Manual**

**ISBN:**979-8356257346

The **Ascension Symptoms Manual** breaks down:

- Physical Symptoms
- Emotional Symptoms
- Mental Symptoms
- Psyche Symptoms
- Light Code Symptoms
- Psychic Abilities
- Plasma Diamond Light Body
- Substances Negatively Enhancing Ascension Symptoms and much more.

All books available on Amazon in Paperback, eBook, and Hardcover

**ISBN:** 9798366416047

On Amazon in
Paperback,
Hardcover, and
eBook

- 144 Lemurian Light Codes
- Meri-Ra-Ka Healing

With messages from Light Masters
from Lemuria, Venus, the Sun, Inner
Earth, the Morana Universe and
more.

# Light Warrior Journals

## Angelic Pearls
## Journal

6 Month Energy Tracker
Journal designed to help you
manage your energy field.

# Illustrations

### Rhea gives Cronus the rock
https://upload.wikimedia.org/wikipedia/commons/9/94/Cronos_and_Rhea_by_Karl_Friedrich_Schinkel.jpg
Karl Friedrich Schinkel; 1781-1841, Public domain, via Wikimedia Commons

### The Pleiades
https://upload.wikimedia.org/wikipedia/commons/f/f8/The_Pleiades_%28Elihu_Vedder%29.jpg
Elihu Vedder, Public domain, via Wikimedia Commons

### Vase of Gudea
https://upload.wikimedia.org/wikipedia/commons/2/29/Girsu_Gudea_libation_vase.jpg
Ernest de Sarzec - Choquin de Sarzec, Ernest (1832-1901), Public domain, via Wikimedia Commons
*Drawing can be found here as well, Wikimedia

### Statuette figurine of a goddess with a horned headdress, possibly Ishtar, Astarte or Nanaya
https://upload.wikimedia.org/wikipedia/commons/d/d3/Statuette_Goddess_Louvre_AO20127.jpg

Louvre Museum, Public domain, via Wikimedia Commons

**Main parts of a mature flower**
https://upload.wikimedia.org/wikipedia/commons/7/7f/Mature_flower_diagram.svg
LadyofHats, Public domain, via Wikimedia Commons

**Drawing of the lion-headed figure found at the Mithraeum of C. Valerius Heracles and sons, dedicated 190 CE at Ostia Antica, Italy**
https://upload.wikimedia.org/wikipedia/commons/5/59/Leontocephaline-Ostia.jpg
See page for author, Public domain, via Wikimedia Commons

**Osiris**
https://upload.wikimedia.org/wikipedia/commons/8/8e/Osiris-tomb-of-Nefertari.jpg
mursal, Public domain, via Wikimedia Commons

**Nefertari**
https://upload.wikimedia.org/wikipedia/commons/d/d7/Maler_der_Grabkammer_der_Nefertari_004.jpg
Maler der Grabkammer der Nefertari, Public domain, via Wikimedia Commons

## Codex Atlanticus

https://upload.wikimedia.org/wikipedia/commons
/6/65/Leonardo_da_Vinci_-
_Codex_Atlanticus_folio_309v_detail1.png
Leonardo da Vinci, Public domain, via Wikimedia
Commons

## Mosaic floor from a bathhouse in Herod's palace

https://upload.wikimedia.org/wikipedia/commons
/9/93/Mosaic_floor_from_a_bathhouse_in_Herod%
27s_palace_-_Google_Art_Project.jpg
Israel Museum, Public domain, via Wikimedia
Commons

## Mnemosyne

https://upload.wikimedia.org/wikipedia/commons
/6/6d/Mnemosyne_%28color%29_Rossetti.jpg
Delaware Art Museum, Samuel and Mary R. Bancroft
Memorial, Public domain, via Wikimedia Commons

## Stage Image

File:Saint eustace.jpg - Wikimedia Commons

## Swastika on the Snoldelev stone

https://upload.wikimedia.org/wikipedia/commons
/f/fd/Snoldelevsunwheel.jpg
No machine-readable author provided.
Bloodofox~commonswiki assumed (based on

copyright claims)., Public domain, via Wikimedia Commons

## Greek Keys

## Pottery Plate of Artemis

## Asgard and the gods

https://upload.wikimedia.org/wikipedia/commons /7/7e/Goddess_Nike_at_Ephesus%2C_Turkey.JPG
Maxfield, Public domain, via Wikimedia Commons

### Nike and Zeus

https://upload.wikimedia.org/wikipedia/commons /6/66/Le_Jupiter_Olympien_ou_l%27art_de_la_scul pture_antique.jpg
Quatremère de Quincy, Public domain, via Wikimedia Commons

### Nike Warrior

https://upload.wikimedia.org/wikipedia/commons /0/02/Nike_warrior_Louvre_Ma969.jpg
Louvre Museum, Public domain, via Wikimedia Commons

### Athena's Birth

https://upload.wikimedia.org/wikipedia/commons /4/42/Amphora_birth_Athena_Louvre_F32.jpg
Louvre Museum, Public domain, via Wikimedia Commons

### Scorpion Men

https://upload.wikimedia.org/wikipedia/commons /4/4d/ScorpionMen.png
Drawn by Faucher-Gudin, from an Assyrian intaglio, Public domain, via Wikimedia Commons

## Soul in Bondage

https://upload.wikimedia.org/wikipedia/commons
/4/4c/Elihu_Vedder_-_Soul_in_Bondage_-
_Google_Art_Project.jpg
Elihu Vedder, Public domain, via Wikimedia
Commons

## Arachne

https://upload.wikimedia.org/wikipedia/commons
/7/7f/Paolo_Veronese_-_Dialettica_-
_Decorazione_del_soffitto_-_Sala_del_Collegio_-
_Palazzo_Ducale_Venezia.jpg
Paolo Veronese, Public domain, via Wikimedia
Commons

## Cybele Plate

File:AiKhanoumPlateSharp.jpg - Wikipedia

## Fortuna

https://upload.wikimedia.org/wikipedia/commons
/1/1a/Allegory_of_Fortune_mg_0010.jpg
Musée des Beaux-Arts de Strasbourg, Public domain,
via Wikimedia Commons

## Morgan le Fay

https://upload.wikimedia.org/wikipedia/commons
/b/bc/Sandys%2C_Frederick_-_Morgan_le_Fay.JPG

Frederick Sandys, Public domain, via Wikimedia Commons

## Persephone-Isis Statue

https://upload.wikimedia.org/wikipedia/commons /c/ce/AMI_-_Isis-Persephone.jpg
Wolfgang Sauber, CC BY-SA 3.0 <https://creativecommons.org/licenses/by-sa/3.0>, via Wikimedia Commons
No Changes made.
Creative Commons — Attribution-ShareAlike 3.0 Unported — CC BY-SA 3.0

## Cupid and Psyche

https://upload.wikimedia.org/wikipedia/commons /a/a6/Gerard_FrancoisPascalSimon-Cupid_Psyche_end.jpg
François Gérard, Public domain, via Wikimedia Commons

# Index

193